W9-AVN-903

30 by 30

A Memoir

The Complete Story

Stephen Pagano

30 by 30

Copyright © 2016 by Stephen Pagano

All rights reserved. No part of this book may be reproduced or transmitted in any form or by any means without written permission of the author.

ISBN (13 digit) 978-1532844461

ISBN (10 digit) 1532844468

This book is dedicated to Frank Allen, Jr and to all those who have passed away throughout our entire adventure.

"It looked like a ballpark. It smelled like a ballpark. It had a feeling and a heartbeat; a personality that was all baseball." - Richie Ashburn on Shibe Park

Philly Fans

Philadelphia is a sports-driven city. It has the most passionate fans in all of sports. It's home to the Phillies, the Eagles, the Flyers, and the 76ers. The fans here hate to lose, to rebuild, or even to hear the phrase "there's always next year." We Philadelphians bleed green, red, and get Flyered-up come the playoffs. We're often known for being both the meanest and the rudest fans in sports. In our time we've booed politicians, thrown snowballs at Santa Claus, and even cheered when Dallas Cowboys star Michael Irvin suffered a career-threatening neck injury at Veterans Stadium. "You play to win the game!" said NFL coach Herm Edwards. They're the words Philadelphia fans live by. Welcome to Philly.

Table of Contents

The Old Ballgame

The Philadelphia Phillies were formed in 1883. They're the oldest continuous one-name team in the history of sports. The Phillies played at Recreation Park at 24th & Ridge Avenue in Philadelphia until 1887. Later that year, they moved to the brand new Baker Bowl, located at Broad & Lehigh. The Baker Bowl opened in 1887 and was notorious for its gigantic 60 foot right field wall, which bore an advertisement on it for Lifebuoy Soap. The Phillies were so bad that fans said, "Even if they got washed with the soap they'd still stink." The Baker Bowl hosted Babe Ruth's final regular season game in 1935, and saw its final games in 1938. It was razed in 1950. The site is now occupied by grocery stores and a car wash.

In 1938 the Philadelphia Phillies moved into Shibe Park, just six blocks away from the Baker Bowl, at 21st & Lehigh. Shibe Park was already home to the Philadelphia Athletics of the American League. The stadium was named after Benjamin Shibe, the owner of the Athletics. On May 16th, 1939 the ballpark hosted the first night game in all American League history. Before the start of the 1953 season, the parks name was changed to Connie Mack Stadium. This name was to honor long-time Athletics coach of 50 years, Connie Mack. The Phillies shared the stadium with the Athletics until 1954. The A's moved to Kansas City in 1955, and then to Oakland in 1968.

A co-worker of mine named Tony has told me when he was a kid; he would attend games at the old ballpark regularly. He vividly remembers the smoke from the cherry cigars in the air. He said, "Even though I was kid, I loved the smell." My father-in-law Ron has told me stories about taking the subway up from South Philly to Broad & Lehigh with friends. They would walk the seven blocks up on Lehigh to 21st street. He said, "The neighborhood was rough, but we wanted to see the Phillies play at Connie Mack Stadium." They were only in elementary school at the time. He also remembers everyone at the game being dressed in business suits with top hats on. Both guys told me that everything was so cheap, from tickets to hot dogs. I love hearing stories about the old ballparks and I really enjoy looking at old black and white photos. I always joke and say If I had a time machine Connie Mack Stadium would be at the top of my list for places to visit. Over the years, the stadium slowly fell apart, and the Phillies were in need of a new home. The city finally build a state-of–the-art ballpark in South Philadelphia, called Veterans Stadium. The Phillies would play their final game at Connie Mack Stadium on

October 1st, 1970. The fans took everything from seats to urinals with them when they left. It was finally demolished in 1976, after being abandoned for six years and nearly burnt down in a fire. A church now inhabits the old ballpark site in North Philadelphia.

The Baker Bowl at Broad & Lehigh

Shibe Park/Connie Mack Stadium at 21st & Lehigh

The Baker Bowl site in 2016

The site of Shibe Park/Connie Mack Stadium in 2016

Bottom of the 9th

Saturday October 23rd, 1993, the Philadelphia Phillies were trailing the Toronto Blue Jays 3 games to 2. The Phillies were in a must-win or go home situation on the road, at the Skydome. The Blue Jays scored three huge runs, in the bottom of the first inning, in front of 53,000 screaming fans. The Phillies finally got on the board in the top of the 4th inning, only for Toronto to add another two runs in the next few innings. At this point it was 5-1 going into the top of the 7th, where the Phillies struck with 5 runs, giving them the lead for the first time in the game, at 6-5. After strong work from David West and Larry Anderson, manager Jim Fregosi decided it was time for closer Mitch Williams, often referred to as "The Wild Thing." Mitch tried to help the Phillies force a game 7 and win their first title since 1980. The lefty Williams walked Ricky Henderson on four straight pitches, giving the Blue Jays a lead-off base runner. Mitch got the next batter, White, to fly out. Paul Molitor then came up, singling to center field, giving the Blue Jays runners on first and second with one out.

Next up was Joe Carter, a name that would haunt me for years to come. After running the count to 2-2, the feared slugger slammed a ball long over the left field fence for a World Series-clinching home run. I remember watching this as a nine year-old boy, upset but not really sure why. I'll never forget the call by Tom Cheeks, the long-time Blue Jays announcer. "Touch 'em all Joe! You'll never hit a bigger home run in your life!" My dad was flipping out, cursing at the television, screaming "You blew it!!" The Blue Jays were back-to-back champions. That's when I became a fan of baseball, and of the Philadelphia Phillies. I couldn't wait to see a game at Veterans Stadium in the 1994 season.

Broad & Pattison

After the 1993 championship run, I was determined to see a game at Veterans Stadium. The Vet, as Philadelphians called it, opened in 1971 in South Philadelphia. The Phillies moved from old Shibe Park, later named Connie Mack Stadium, which was knocked down in 1976. I begged my dad to take me and my brother Mark to a game in 1994. In early May he purchased us tickets to our first Phillies game. We walked up Broad Street on that cool spring night, in short-sleeves Phillies shirts and blue jeans. Police officers controlled the traffic lights in order to help the flow of cars move more smoothly. People honked their horns at each other as they waited to enter the parking lot. Mark and I were excited to see the game. I remember seeing "The Vet" carved out in the grass just outside the stadium. Just across the street we saw The Spectrum, "America's Showplace." It had been home to the Flyers and the 76ers since 1967.

Fans swarmed the entrance, dressed head-to-toe in their Phillies gear. We walked up the long ramps and handed the Phillies attendant our tickets. He glanced at our tickets, saying, "You guys are in the 500 level. Take the ramp up to your left and follow the signs." We thanked him and went up towards our seats. The aroma of fresh peanuts, popcorn and hot dogs found my young nose. The first time I saw the field, my eyes lit up with excitement. The beloved iconic Phillie Phanatic was dancing on top of the home dugout, entertaining fans before the game started. I saw the many levels of Veterans Stadium, distinguished with different colored seats. The 700 level had yellow; lower ones were red and brown. On the stadium speakers, I heard Phillies PA announcer Dan Baker say, "Ladies & Gentlemen! Welcome to beautiful Veterans Stadium and we thank you for coming."

During the game we cheered on the Phillies in our red attire. Catcher Darren Daulton would hit a home run to deep right centerfield. The crowd went nuts, as fans gave high fives to each other. I turned to my dad and said, "What I miss?" He replied, "When the ball clears the fence in fair territory it's a home run." Mark and I both nodded as we now understood everyone's excitement. "Oh like what Joe Carter did in the World Series last year?" I said. He smirked and said, "Don't bring that up again." The 1994 season was cut short do to the players strike. The Phillies never got a chance to return to the Fall Classic that year. Other Phillies teams couldn't match the magic of that 1993 National League Championship team, and it was like that for a very long time.

As the 1995 season rolled around, I was looking forward to attending more games at The Vet. A neighborhood friend named Jay Capaldi told me and my brother about getting players' autographs before and after Phillies home games. I said, "Can we do that? It's free?" He said, "Yeah everyone does it! It's so much fun! You guys should come." So Mark and I agreed, and that's when The Vet became a second home. We spent all summer down there. I remember that's all I cared about; I couldn't even focus in school. All I wanted to do was to chase players around, hounding them for their John Hancock. We organized our binders full of baseball cards and photos for every visiting team. That time really changed my life. It's a hobby I still practice today at age 31, collecting autographs from sports athletes and celebrities. Mark and I spent many late nights at The Vet. I remember calling my dad from the payphones regularly around 11pm, to come pick us up after games in the summer time.

We were extra excited for the 1996 season, because The Vet was hosting the 67th Major League all-star game, their first since 1976. Veterans Stadium replaced all of their old seats with brand-new blue ones in preparation for the event. The greatest players from the National League and from the American League competed in this exhibition game. The week before Mark and I even attended the All Star Fest, held at the Convention Center in Center City. That included many baseball activities, with batting cages, fan photos, and getting to run around replica stadium bases.

On Sunday July 8th, 1996, Mark and I bought tickets for the Home Run Derby. This was an event where star players faced off to see who could hit the most home runs. I remember Barry Bonds shattered his bat in the second round, and we were just one row short of getting it. Bonds and McGwire would smash home runs into the upper deck all day long. We watched Barry Bonds defeat Mark McGwire in the final round to win the trophy. The next night The Vet hosted the "Summer Classic", as baseball fans referred to it. Phillies greats Mike Schmidt, Richie Ashburn, Jim Bunning, Steve Carlton, and Robin Roberts all threw out the ceremonial first pitch. The National League would shut out the American League 6-0 in St. Louis great Ozzie Smith's final all star game. Norristown native Mike Piazza won the MVP award for the National League.

In 1998, Mark McGwire would go on to break the single season home run record of 61, until then held by Roger Maris. He ended up with 70 that year. By 2001, Bonds would also break Mark McGwire's single season home run record of 70, with 73. In 2007, Barry Bonds would go on to be the all-time home run champ with 762, breaking Hank Aaron's record of 755. Both players have since been linked with PED use, but I still think Barry Bonds should be in the Hall of Fame in Cooperstown. That was a special year, and I was becoming a bigger baseball fan as the seasons passed. Mark & I, bought cheap tickets to every game, which almost invariably put us in the infamous 700 level. The 700 level of The Vet was known for both the rudest and the most passionate fans in all of baseball. Veterans Stadium actually had a holding cell, with a real judge, for fans who misbehaved themselves. We were too young for all of that; we just wanted to be at the game at the cheapest price. I remember filling out my scorecard in that upper deck in so many regular season games.

One of my favorite stories from The Vet was when Phillies all star relief pitcher Ricky Bottalico threw his glove into the stands at the end of the 1998 season. That glove hit my chest and then landed on top of the Phillies dugout. I leaned over and grabbed it. My brother couldn't believe that I got it. After the game, I had Ricky sign the glove. As he did that, he said to me, "I made a mistake! I need this back." My face dropped, but he said, "Joking." I regret selling that glove to this day. Occasionally, I'll check eBay for it to see if someone has it for sale.

Mark and I would continue going down The Vet for a few more years, until the time we started high school. That's when I lost interest in the game a little, from about 2002-2005. My final game at the ballpark was on September 27th, 2001, my 17th birthday. It was a Larry Bowa bobblehead giveaway night, which I still own. One of my biggest regrets is not having attended any of the final games at the old ball park, which closed in 2003. On March 21st, 2004 Veterans Stadium was finally imploded. Later on that day, I went down to the site and took a rock home for a souvenir. Years later I bought a pair of those blue seats, which I still have in my basement today. In total I saw over 200 games there. I learned and grew up with baseball at rugged old Veterans Stadium, corner of Broad and Pattison.

Veterans Stadium – 1971-2003

My Summer Home

The 700 Level

Broad & Pattison

My Veterans Stadium Seats

Home Plate at the former site of Veterans Stadium

30/30 Vison

It was Saturday May 18th, 2013 and almost game time. The Minnesota Twins were getting ready to host the Boston Red Sox on a cloudy evening in downtown Minneapolis. It was 68 degrees, and we were hoping they went on with the game, because there was rain in the forecast. We never experienced a rain-out in seven years of traveling and we didn't want this to be our first. As we approached this fairly new stadium, we had our tickets in hand. I turned to Jay, Pat & Steve and said "this is crazy" and they responded right off, "I know, this is amazing." We weren't referring to the game itself, or to the hot dogs, the beer, or the great seats. We were talking about Target Field. For everyone else, including the players, this was just a regular season game with not a lot of meaning at all. But for us this was our 30th and final baseball stadium visited in all of the Major Leagues, and all by the age of 30. A journey we started way back in 2006, this was an adventure that took us across the country, for baseball. This is the story of four guys from South Philadelphia who saw a game in all 30 Major League stadiums during the best era in Philadelphia Phillies history.

Batter Up!

P at Lerro, Jason Pinto, Steven Grosso and I were all born and raised in South Philadelphia. We lived just two miles from the sports complex our whole lives. We grew up in the same neighborhood and came from the same Italian background. We played stickball in the streets, and mimicked some of our favorite baseball players, with their unique batting stances. We played catch with our fathers and with our friends in the middle of narrow Philly streets, holding up traffic. We sledded down the ramps at The Vet during massive snowstorms in the winter. We played tackle football at Marconi Park and fished with our dads down The Lakes. We played pick-up games of basketball at Jenks schoolyard and the field at 18th & Johnson. There was always something special about the fireworks on July 4th every summer at Veterans Stadium. We enjoyed all sports movies growing up, but especially Rookie of the Year, Little Big League, A League of Their Own, and The Sandlot. We all wanted to be like Benny "The Jet" Rodriguez and "tackle the beast". We ran up the steps of the Art Museum just like Rocky Balboa did. We argued who had better steaks, Geno's, Pat's, or Jim's on South Street. We enjoyed water ice and pretzel sticks from Pop's, John's and Italiano's on hot summer nights. We loved our soft pretzels and Primo's hoagies. We enjoyed eating Tastykakes while walking up the Italian Market on 9th street. We had fun taking school field trips to the Liberty Bell and to the Franklin Institute. That was growing up in South Philly.

Over the years I saw Steve and Jay both at school and in the neighborhood. They occasionally also rode their bikes down by The Vet, and I would see them there. We talked nonstop about sports, video games, and professional wrestling. I didn't meet Pat until July of 2005, but we instantly hit it off. In the summer of 2006, our girlfriends Alana and Jackie were best friends, so we hung out often. A month later, I spoke to Pat about possibly going to New York to see the Yankees play some time. He agreed to look into it and to let me know. Pat bought tickets for us to see a game in August of 2006. Unfortunately it was raining on game day, so we didn't go. The Yankees played the game anyway, so Pat couldn't get a refund. I told him I would make it up to him and buy his ticket next time around.

Near Labor Day in 2006, I saw Steve in the neighborhood and we spoke about the state of the Phillies, amongst other things. I told him that Pat and I were going to Yankee Stadium in a few weeks. Voice full of excitement, he said, "You're kidding me? Jay and I have been dying to see a game there." I told him I would see what I could do and get back to him. He said, "Great!"

After a week or so I called Steve and told him that I had been able to get four tickets together in the bleachers at Yankee Stadium, for a game against the Red Sox. He was beyond happy and said Jay would be too. On Sunday September 17th, Pat picked all of us up for our first trip to Yankee Stadium. That trip changed our lives forever. We thought this was a one-time thing. Boy, were we wrong.

161st Street

September 17, 2006 was a chilly night in the Bronx, NY at Yankee Stadium. The Boston Red Sox were in town, the Yankees bitter division rival for ages. I remember taking the NJ Transit train in with the guys that day, finally arriving at NYC's Penn Station. We eventually took an expensive cab ride from there to the stadium, instead of using the subway, which we weren't familiar with back then. Little did I know we could have jumped on the D train to the Bronx for just a few bucks, and saved some time avoiding gridlocked New York traffic. We were in our early 20's, enjoying life in the Big Apple, the city that never sleeps. We had talked about this trip for weeks, and now it was finally here. "Baseball in prime time!" Jay said. "Nothing like the Sox & Yanks as the baseball game of the week on ESPN!" I grinned. The guys said jokingly, "These tickets better not be fake; we came all the way out here." I smirked and said, "Relax, we'll be fine." To be honest I was a little nervous, because I had never purchased tickets online before. But as soon as they scanned them and we got in, I felt a lot better.

We walked through the turnstiles in the bleacher section on 161st street in the Bronx. The atmosphere was alive and buzzing. It felt like a playoff game, with fans of both teams yelling and screaming at each other in that heated September division game. The stadium lights were bright, bearing down on this baseball palace. I remember we were a little disappointed because the bleacher seats were alcohol free, and because we were confined to just that area of the ballpark. After a minute or so, we just grabbed some food and headed to our seats. "We're here to watch baseball, not drink, so we'll be ok!" Steve said. I laughed and said, "You're right! Let's have some fun and enjoy this" as I sipped my soda and ate my soft pretzel. I'm guessing the older stadiums were like that, so that you couldn't buy a cheap ticket, then sneak down to better seats. I was saying, "It wasn't like that at The Vet. They would have just let you sit anywhere at any time!" "I guess that's what winning baseball games does for you," the guys replied. I was just happy to be at Yankee Stadium, a place I dreamed of visiting when I was a little kid in South Philly. This was the place where legends like Mickey Mantle, Babe Ruth, Roger Maris, Joe DiMaggio, and Lou Gehrig once played, and I was thinking to myself, "Now we're here!"

The air was damp. Peanuts, and hot dog wrappers covered the ground below us. I could almost see playoff aspirations in the players' eyes. Derek Jeter and Alex Rodriguez were both stretching around shortstop before the game. I had never been in a baseball environment like that before, so I was really surprised by the intensity from the fans. A Red Sox fan yelled, "Yankees suck", and he was immediately booed by the home crowd. I remember really taking it all in, as I gazed out and around the old stadium, like a kid at Christmas looking at his tree with a load of presents under it. We were only a few feet away from famous Monument Park, and the plaques of the greatest Yankees of all time were inside.

Yankee Stadium was constructed in 1923, and was often referred to as "The House that Ruth Built." I was thinking that the Yankees had won so many championships in their franchise over the years and we only had the one from 1980, before I was even born. They had won 26 championships up to that point, pretty much dominating the century. But the Yankees ended up losing this game, the second of a doubleheader that day, 5-4. We headed back home on the train shortly after that, with fond memories of the Cathedral in the Bronx. Both Yankees and Red Sox fans packed the train back to Manhattan after the game. All the guys said that it had been a lot of fun and that we should do it again sometime. I replied, "Definitely!" None of us knew what was on deck next, as we prepared for a journey of a lifetime.

Pat, Steve, & Jay in the bleacher seats at Yankee Stadium

Me & Jay in the bleacher seats at 161st Street in the Bronx

Our Rookie Season

On January 23, 2007 the Phillies veteran shortstop Jimmy Rollins said that the Phillies were the team to beat in the National League East. This put a lot of pressure on a young team, but really excited fans who were starving for the playoffs after a 14-year hiatus. This came after the Phillies had finished 12 games behind the Division-winning New York Mets in the previous season. The 2007 off-season was a busy one for me. When we left Yankee Stadium the previous September, I promised the guys that I would look into more baseball stadium trips. I figured we would start with something simple within easy driving range, like Oriole Park at Camden Yards in Baltimore. I remember calling Steve up on my Razr phone sometime in February, asking "Would you want to take a road trip down to Camden Yards?" Steve said, "Definitely! I'll tell Jay." I said, "Great I'll tell Pat, maybe he'll drive us." Pat had the newest car out of the bunch, so we figured it was the safest bet. I also told Steve I wanted to return to Yankee Stadium, but this time with better seats, so we could walk around and see the entire stadium. He agreed wholeheartedly. After I confirmed with Pat and Steve talked to Jay, we had our first trip set. A few weeks into March, I was also able to find us some affordable outfield seats at Yankee Stadium. These weren't bleacher seats, so they gave us access to the whole park, which all the guys were really happy with. "We can even drink in those seats." I said. Now we had two trips planned, but we still had not even the slightest clue that we would end up seeing all thirty stadiums.

On April 14th, 2007 we ventured out on our first road trip of the new season. Pat picked us up at my parents' house at 10th & Wolf in South Philly around 4pm, and then we took Interstate 95 south toward Baltimore. The Weather Channel was calling for thunderstorms all night, but we were hoping they would get the game in. Little did we know, this would be the closest we would come to a rain-out. On the ride down, Pat tuned his satellite radio to a station we liked. Along the way, we talked about our Yankee Stadium trip from last year, and how we were excited to see the ballpark again in a month. Pat's GPS exclaimed, "Right turn ahead." It took us approximately one hour and forty minutes to get there, stopping once in Delaware for gas. To our left through the raininy skies and barley visible was M&T Bank Stadium, home of the Baltimore Ravens. The stadiums purple seats illuminated as a lightning bolt filled the sky.

Once we arrived in Baltimore, Pat parked right outside the stadium. The large sign outside said "Oriole Park". The Orioles were playing the Kansas City Royals that night. We noticed the dark clouds, and immediately felt drizzle on our new Orioles hats. In the beginning we wore the home team's hat, unless the Phillies were playing. I snapped a quick picture of the front of the ballpark and then we proceeded to the gates. I always wore my backpack, in case any of us wanted to buy souvenirs. The guys said, "I hope they play this game, we drove all this way." Once inside we were able to get a group picture with the Orioles Mascot, Oriole the Bird, despite all the kids around him. The Orioles had many shops that were connected to old B&O Warehouse in right field. I bought a few postcards, which I collected throughout, and a magnet for my mother's refrigerator. "I've seen this on television and in PlayStation games," I said. "I think Ken Griffey, Jr. once hit this building in a Home Run Derby," Jay said. As I approached, I saw that there was a labeled brick saying just that, so I pulled out my new digital camera and took a picture of it. I also pointed out that Camden Yards was used in the movie "Major League 2", starring Charlie Sheen.

As we walked around the concourse packed with eager fans of all ages, I noticed the Orioles' staff giving out orange ponchos. As a joke I took one and wore it for a while, though it actually came in handy later on in the game. The aroma of French fries, cheeseburgers, and hot dogs filled the air, making our hungry stomachs rumble more. We grabbed some food from the concessions, along with a few Bud Lights. Ushers cleaned off the green seats with a white towel, as fans found their seats in the lower levels. They removed the saturated tarp from the field, and shortly after that the National Anthem was sung. We took off our hats out of respect for our country, then walked around for a little more, dodging the light raindrops. I said, "I wish we had time to see the Baltimore Harbor." The Harbor is beautiful, with many shops and restaurants sitting right on top of the water for people to visit.

We finally went to our seats in the Hall of Fame club around the second inning. Our seats were dry, as we were underneath the second level of the stadium. I enjoyed the game, thinking about all that Cal Ripken, Jr. aka "The Iron Man" had accomplished here. He played in 2,632 consecutive games, breaking Lou Gehrig's record streak that many people thought was unbreakable. I remember getting Cal's autograph back on June 8th, 1998. It was my eight grade dinner dance at the Holiday Inn on 10th & Pattison. Just before the game, my childhood friend Jay Capaldi and I went to batting practice at Veterans Stadium in our dress clothes. Ripken signed every fan on the first base side that night. He was always a class act.

Later on in the game we all snuck down to the third base line, which was not occupied, and sat there. I instantly had flashbacks to The Vet, because I was sitting so close without legit tickets. A foul ball buzzed by our heads and shot right behind us. Jay and I chased the ball down only to come up short. Another fan picked it up with joy and excitement in his face. Baltimore beat the Royals that night 6-4. On the ride back Pat fought through some fierce weather in his car. We joked and said, "It looked like a hurricane." I said, "It looked like The Wizard of Oz." We had a good time, but we all were already anxious to head back to New York to see the Yankees play in just a few weeks.

On Saturday May 26th, 2007 the Yankees were getting ready to take on the Anaheim Angels. We were excited to head back "To The House that Ruth Built". Once we arrived at Penn Station, we walked just a few blocks to the subway station and took the train that said D to the Bronx. I said, "We're not spending $60 on a cab this time." We purchased our round-trip MetroCards, and off we went, back to the stadium that we just visited eight months prior. I remember the subway operator said, "Next stop, Yankee Stadium." We rapidly jumped up to prepare for our stop. The train was packed with excited Yankees fans, eager to see the "Bronx Bombers." A loud squeal followed as the train operator applied the brakes. As the subway doors opened, we were hit with the smell of urine. The Bronx approached us, and we got off the train in our white tees, sunglasses, and Yankees hats. A homeless man asked us for change on the way up the steps to the stadium. We dug in our pockets and gave him all the loose quarters we had.

The weather was fantastic on that beautiful Memorial Day weekend. Many people had flocked down the shore, but here we were at Yankee Stadium. We walked around the front of the building to the main entrance. Across the street I saw the walkway that said "26 time World Champions." I saw the large bat outside, a staple of the iconic arena. Once inside we explored the entire stadium, this time around. We could smell fresh nachos and ballpark franks lingering around the concourse. Our mouths watered in hunger, since we didn't eat breakfast. We grabbed some lunch from the concessions, along with some $8 cold draft Miller Lite's. Pat said, "Finally a beer at Yankee Stadium." I just remember thinking to myself that as old and run down as the place was, it was so historical.

I was just as excited this time around being there as last season. We found our seats in the outfield after squeezing through a packed house of Yankees and Angels fans. The fans cheered for the home team and booed the opposition all through the game. The Yankees faithful were tough on the Angels players without pause. The Yankees lost that game 3-1. Just across the street we could see the new Yankee Stadium rising up as we boarded our subway train back to Manhattan.

Afterwards we visited famous Times Square on 42nd street for a little bit. All of the bright lights bounced off each building as hundreds of yellow taxis sped through the intersection. Horns honked as traffic backed up and pedestrians crossed the streets of the popular tourist attraction. I said, "I love Times Square; it might be my favorite place ever." I always wanted to go there for New Year's Eve. We took a cab to 112th and Broadway outside Tom's Restaurant. It was famous for the exterior shots of our favorite sitcom, "Seinfeld". Yada, yada, yada we snapped some photos and headed to dinner in Little Italy.

As we walked up Mulberry Street I could smell Italian food in the air. Italian flags flapped in the light wind as they hung from the second and third story balconies. Colored lights lined up the walls of many of the old buildings. The guys looked up and said, "I love the fire escapes! They are so New York." Italian music was playing outside as the sun came down. Steve said, "Donnie Brasco was filmed up here." I told him I love that movie. We decided on eating at Pellegrino's. It was a very authentic Italian place with some great choices. The busboy brought us bread, as the waiter took our order.

Chatter filled the restaurant as people scanned the menus. Jay and Steve ordered bruschetta. Pat and I ordered fried calamari as appetizers. Eventually our dinner arrived, consisting of pasta, chicken parmesan, and ravioli. After we rubbed our stomachs signaling we were full, the waiter asked if we wanted dessert. We all glanced at each other, and somehow squeezed in some delicious New York cheesecake and tiramisu. We headed home after that. On the train back I said to the fellas, "We gotta do Fenway Park next." Excitement in their eyes and voices, the guys all told me to look it up, and book it!

The next day I did search airfare and hotel websites for Boston as promised. As I gathered my information, I thought to myself maybe we could squeeze in one more NYC trip this summer. It's cheap, fun, and it's New York! But I didn't want to do another Yankee Stadium trip. That would've been three times in one year, and I wanted a little variety. So I started checking the New York Mets schedule for August, because I was looking at Boston trips for the beginning of September. I found cheap tickets to Shea Stadium for a Saturday night. I immediately called Steve up, almost shaking in excitement, and said, "Yo, what's going?" He replied, "What you got for me, man? Boston?" I said, "I'll get to that in a moment." He said, "Come on man, you're killing me." I asked him what he thought of Shea Stadium in August and Fenway Park in September. We agreed to phone the guys, who were all in. I was able to find us a cheap nonstop flight to Boston Logan airport, and also a nice hotel about five miles away from Fenway Park, for about $200 per person. The catch was that the game tickets were $100 each. Later we realized that those tickets would be priceless after the game. Despite the expense, everyone agreed and our amazing 2007 rookie season continued.

Just a few weeks after we left New York, I realized we haven't all attended a game at Citizens Bank Park together. Although we had all seen many games there separately, we decided it was time to do one together. Tickets were quite easy to acquire, and it was just a short 10-minute walk from our houses. On June 16th around 6pm, we set forth to see the Phillies host the Detroit Tigers, in this exciting interleague game.

Citizens Bank Park opened in 2004, after the Phillies played 32 seasons at The Vet. It was nice to have a home ballpark with real grass, after having all those years with that dreadful AstroTurf. Overall, the stadium is just a beautiful design. There isn't a bad seat in the house; even the upper levels have great views. The sights of William Penn, the Comcast building and the Liberty Place towers filled up our stellar skyline in the distance. The smell of cheesesteaks and Chickie's and Pete's Crab Fries filled the air. We grabbed both as we walked around Ashburn Alley. It was named after the legendary Phillies Hall of Fame player and commentator Richie Ashburn, also known as "Whitey", who passed away in 1997. I said to the guys, "I got his autograph in 1996 at The Vet. I remember listening to Richie and to Harry Kalas call games on TV as a kid. They were a great combo."

We took a group picture together, then headed over to our right field seats. Our fun and lovable mascot, the Phillie Phanatic, was dancing on the field. His bright green costume lit up underneath the ballpark lights. The stadium was half-filled on that humid summer night. Many fans wore their Chase Utley, and Jimmy Rollins t-shirts to the game. I remember a fan had a sign that said, "Thanks for Polanco." Placido Polanco played for the Phillies, from 2002-2005. He became an all star 3rd baseman for the tigers, after we traded him. The fans cheered loud, after every Phillies player reached base. The Phillies won that game 6-3. The stadium erupted in cheers and high fives from an impressive victory. As we were leaving, Jay reached under his seat to set down his beer, and saw an envelope. He opened it, and said, "Wow! A hundred bucks!" I said, "This must be our lucky night, maybe our lucky year." After the game, we all headed down to Atlantic City. Jay split the money four ways, and we had a good time. I said, "Next up, Queens."

On August 11th, 2007 we did our normal travel routine to Manhattan. The Mets were playing the Florida Marlins at Shea Stadium. We took NJ Transit up to Penn Station, our ears popping along the way. It was a hot and sticky day in New York, around 90 degrees. Before the game we took a taxi over to Battery Park to see the Statue of Liberty. The line was huge to purchase tickets. I was a little sneaky and was able to cut in front of some school kids on a class trip, to save us some time. The small overcrowded ferry then took us over to Liberty Island. The water slammed on the sides of the ferry, as our bodies rocked back and forth. We snapped some pictures of Lady Liberty, as a light breeze came off the Hudson River. We could see the famous Brooklyn and Manhattan Bridges in the distance. I told the guys, "One day I wanna walk them." The beautiful New York City skyline caught our eyes from the island. We reflected on the vicious attacks that happened just six years prior on 9/11. We hopped back on the ferry as it was less crowded this time. Ellis Island was our next stop. "Many of our ancestors came through this very port." Steve said. After about an hour of doing all that, we decided it was game time. A few people told me we could take the seven train or even the Long Island Railroad to Queens. We figured a taxi would be the quickest, since we didn't want to be late for the game. The cab driver pulled up to the ballpark and said in faltering English, "This is Shea Stadium, $18 dollars please." We gave him $22 and thanked him nicely.

As we arrived outside Shea, I quickly noticed its similarity to Veterans Stadium. It was old, circular and falling apart. Shea Stadium opened in 1964, and was set to be razed in 2008. That's why I really wanted to do it, because it wouldn't be around much longer, and just to say we did it. It really was just a throw-in trip before our big weekend in Boston. The Mets were hosting the Flordia Marlins that night. We kept our tradition going, wearing the home team hat, but inside it killed us because we were diehard Phillies fans since we were kids. At that time the Mets were leading the division by a comfortable margin, and the Phillies had been just hanging around all year. Jimmy Rollins was eating his words at the moment. The Mets fans were intense the whole game, rooting for their first place team. We were hoping for a late season collapse that would get us into the playoffs for the first time in 14 years.

As we wandered around the concourse the smell of popcorn, hot dogs and burgers wafted up our noses. The heat was letting up a little bit as the sun went down in Queens, but our Mets hats were still soaked with sweat. We found our seats along the third baseline and I asked another fan to take a picture for us. We could see brand new Citi Field being built over the left field fence. I said, "That's supposed to open in 2009." The Mets had a huge scoreboard in right center field. We were hardcore scoreboard watching, to see what the Phillies were doing back home. I pointed to the Big Apple in the center and said, "That goes off every time someone hits a home run." We walked around a little, Jay grabbed his dad a t-shirt, Pat grabbed a shot glass, and I got a postcard. After the game we all agreed that we hated the Mets, and we hoped they choked down the stretch. Many people tell us how lucky we are to see a game there, now that it's long gone. Flordia won that game 7-5. As we headed back home that night, the only thing that was on all of our minds was Fenway Park.

It was September 1st, 2007 in Philadelphia as we loaded up the trunk of a cab and told the driver to head to Philadelphia International Airport. The weather was in the 70's and a little muggy. The guys were anxious to get to Boston and finally see a game at historic Fenway Park. The stadium opened on April 19th, 1912, just a week after the famous ocean liner Titanic hit an iceberg in the middle of the North Atlantic. My whole life I had dreamed of seeing a baseball game at Fenway. I remember watching the movie "Fever Pitch" in 2004, and saying "I want to go there!"

Our flight was short and quick as we arrived at Boston Logan around 3pm. We took a 20-minute cab ride from the airport to the Courtyard Marriott hotel and checked in. The hotel clerk said, "Can I help you sir?" I said, "Yes, checking in, the last name is Pagano." She replied, "Yes, we have you staying one night, two double beds, non smoking correct?" I said, "Correct!" as I scribbled my signature on the papers, and handed over my Capital One credit card. We dropped our bags on the neatly made beds, and felt the cool air from the noisy air conditioner in the wall. We grabbed some food at a local Applebee's and discussed the night ahead of us. The restaurant was filled with Boston sports memorabilia, New England Patriots and Boston Celtics championship newspapers and banners especially. The guys said, "Tonight is gonna be great! I agreed. We paid our check, and then quickly jumped in a taxi to Fenway Park. The cab driver asked where we'd come from and we all said, "Philadelphia" at the same time. He said, "Oh, great! You're gonna enjoy Fenway Park!"

I could see the historical ballpark in the distance. We thanked our driver and proceeded to the entrance. Before we went in we took a picture with the Ted Williams statue outside of the stadium. Ted Williams was one of the greatest players in history, being the only guy ever to bat .400 for an entire season. He also won two Triple Crowns. He is in the Baseball Hall of Fame. We gave the Red Sox attendant our tickets, which had Boston catcher Jason Varitek on them. They scanned with no problem and in his Boston accent he said, "Enjoy the game!" So we headed into the stadium. We grabbed some Fenway Franks and a couple of cold beers, then we headed to Yawkey Way. It's a street connected to the ballpark where all the fans hang out and enjoy themselves. Many souvenir and Boston Red Sox team stores fill the area, as well as food vendors, and previous championship banners. We made our way over to the grandstand to our seats. I could see the bright stadium lights over the Monster, as night time approached. The first time I saw the Green Monster I was amazed. I just remember all the guys saying, "Wow!" I said out loud, "This is a true home field advantage." The large Citgo sign was visible in left center field. The right field fence is a lot lower near Pesky's pole. The pole is named after Johnny Pesky, a former Red Sox 2nd baseman. Boston players David Ortiz, Dustin Pedroia, and Manny Ramirez were all signing autographs along the first base side for kids before the start of the game. We sat in our tiny, uncomfortable wooden seats just between home plate and first base. I said, "People must have been smaller back when this place opened." The guys laughed. Steve said, "Maybe we'll see Stephen King here. I know he comes to a lot of games at Fenway." The peanut vendor came to our section a few times and yelled, "Peanuts here! Get your fresh peanuts." Jay said, "I'll take a pack." The vendor threw the pack like a baseball toward us, and Jay passed the money down the aisle.

We walked around the concourse a few more times and then stopped at the restroom. The bathrooms are pretty unique at the old ballparks. Many have troughs, which are large sinks that men urinate in. It was weird, but old school at the same time. Pat grabbed us another round a beers before we headed back to the seats. I lifted up my Red Sox hat as I scratched my head and said, "I can't believe we're at Fenway Park." They nodded their heads in agreement. When we returned, Jay noticed something on the scoreboard. Without actually saying what it meant, he said, "Look! Nothing but goose eggs in the hit column." In baseball terms that means zero, and we instantly knew what was going on, six innings into that game at Fenway Park. Clay Buchholz of the Boston Red Sox, in just his second big league start, was throwing a no-hitter. I remember a fan saying, "It just showed up on ESPN, no hitter alert in Boston." We all said, "Damn it!" I hope they don't jinx it!" I was thinking to myself how crazy would this be to witness a no no at Fenway Park. The sold out crowd sang "Sweet Caroline" as it blasted from the stadium speakers. It was a Neil Diamond smash hit and Red Sox tradition.

In the final three innings, with every pop up or ground out, the crowd moaned and groaned, hoping to see history. The players and the fans were extremely nervous and on edge. "I never seen a no-hitter in person before." I said. Then with two outs in the top of the 9th inning, rookie Clay Buchholz caught Nick Markakis looking at 1-2 curveball to compete his no-hitter. Everyone jumped up and down, screaming and hollering. Fenway Park was shaking. The guys all said at the same time, "It feels like we won the World Series." Then I thought to myself, "That will never happen. But I'll never forget this game ever!" I never heard a stadium that loud in my life. Fans exited the park, cheering and hollering in celebration. Steve said, "I can't believe we just witnessed a no-hitter at Fenway Park." We hung outside the ballpark for a few hours and enjoyed some cold drinks at the local bars. It was tough to go to bed as our adrenaline was pumping, and we had so much energy from the game.

On our flight home I said to the guys, "I should look up a trip to Chicago so we can see the Cubs play at Wrigley Field in a few weeks." I was partly joking, but all the guys said, "Do it!" at the same time. That gave me more motivation to get it done. They relied on me at this point to call them with good news, so we could keep the train rolling. Then I had this crazy idea. What if we just flew to Chicago for the day and skipped a hotel? It could save us some money, since we'd already spent a lot this year on travel and game tickets. I was skeptical at first, because this was asking a lot from the guys. Fortunately, after I pitched this wacky idea to the guys, they immediately agreed. I remember them saying, "We just wanted to do another trip no matter what the crazy circumstances were." So I booked us a roundtrip flight arriving at Chicago O'Hare International Airport around 10:30am and departing Chicago around 9pm that same night. The guys didn't care about staying over this time; they just wanted to see the game.

On September 22, 2007, exactly three weeks after the history we saw in Boston, we were on a flight to Chicago. We were going to see the Cubs play the Pirates at Wrigley Field, in the Windy City. Our flight was a little bumpy; our drinks went bouncing off the snack trays a few times. The airline pilot reminded us to keep our seatbelts on. Once we landed, we took a taxi right to the ballpark. I was getting a little sick in the backseat from the speeding cab, but I knew I would feel a lot better as soon as I saw the stadium. I remember many shops outside, and plenty of people selling Cubs memorabilia all over. We walked on Waveland, and on Sheffield Avenue where many Sammy Sosa home run balls had landed over the years. We had lunch across the street, at Harry Caray's tavern, named after the legendary broadcaster who passed away in 1998. They had a statue of him outside of the stadium, where I took a picture before heading inside. The guys said, "He was the best at singing 'Take Me Out to the Ball Game'." I snapped a picture of the front of the stadium on my new iphone which just came out. The guy at the Apple store told me that this phone would change everything. I said, "Yeah, We'll see."

Once inside, we couldn't wait to the see the ivy. It was bright green, and it covered the entire outfield wall. I remember seeing it as a kid in video games and in movies. I said, "If a ball lands in there at any point in the game it's an automatic ground rule double." We wandered around the concourse for a little bit, then headed to our seats in section 213. The rooftop seats across the street were packed with Cubs fans. Wrigley Field was in really good condition, just like Fenway Park. A nice breeze hit our faces as we sat down and ate in our seats. I said, "Hey, it is the Windy City."

We stopped at a concession to get some ice cream, and asked for some Jimmies on top. The nice African-American lady working there said, "What are Jimmies?" We laughed and said, "We're not in South Philly." The guys said, "It looks great here for being almost 100 years old." I said, "I can't believe it opened in 1914." As I adjusted my Cubs hat, I couldn't help but notice the old scoreboards all around. Wrigley Field and Fenway Park are the last two stadiums that have their scoreboards changed by hand. We had a great time inside the "Friendly Confines of Wrigley Field." I couldn't wait for the seventh inning stretch. The stadium announcer called,

"Take me out to the ball game,
Take me out with the crowd;
Just buy me some peanuts and Cracker Jack,
I don't care if I never get back.
Let me root, root, root for the Cubbies
If they don't win, it's a shame.
For its one, two, three strikes, you're out,
At the old ball game."

I said, "That was great, let's check out the rest of the city while we have some time. The Cubs won the game 9-5. After the game, we walked around downtown Chicago in The Loop area for a little bit. Eventually we ended up at Soldier Field, home of the Chicago Bears, where Jay even tried to sneak onto the field before security chased him away. We all had a good laugh after a really long day. After that it was time to head back to the airport and home to Philly. We were exhausted, but had a great day trip to Chicago.

Our flight touched down around midnight our time. We had managed to see the three classic stadiums -- Yankee Stadium, Fenway Park, and Wrigley Field -- all in one year. Some baseball fans don't do that in a lifetime, I thought. I was very proud of this accomplishment, but we had no clue this was something that would continue. I really believed we would just see the older stadiums. But everyone said, "There is no reason why we can't continue to do this." That was all I needed to hear, and 2008 would be just as special. But little did we know how special.

The New York Mets would complete one of the biggest collapses in baseball history. They were up 7 games with 17 games to play, but the Phillies would overtake them and win the division on the last day of the season. Our first post-season berth in 14 years. Jimmy Rollins bold statement, "We're the team to beat!" rang true. We would go on to get swept in the first round of the playoffs by the red-hot Colorado Rockies. The Rockies would eventually lose to the Boston Red Sox in the World Series, the Sox capturing their second title in four seasons.

Me & Jay at Camden Yards in Baltimore

Me, Jay, Steve and Pat with the Oriole Bird

Yankee Stadium

Jay, Steve, Pat & Me at Yankee Stadium

Seinfeld Restaurant

Times Square

Little Italy in New York

Mulberry Street

Citizens Bank Park

Me, Jay, Steve and Pat in Ashburn Alley

Me, Steve, Jay and Pat at Shea Stadium

Shea Stadium Scoreboard

Stephen Pagano

New York City skyline from Liberty Island

Ellis Island in New York City

Yawkey Way at Fenway Park

The Ted Williams statue outside Fenway Park

Fenway Park in Boston

No Hitter at Fenway Park on 9/1/07

Wrigley Field in Chicago

Me, Jay, Pat and Steve at Wrigley Field

Chicago Skyline

Soldier Field – Home of the Chicago Bears

On the Road to Victory

I was really excited when the 2008 schedule came out. I decided we had to see the Phillies play on the road this year, especially being the new National League East Champs. I started thinking like a General Manager would. I had to manage our money and time well. I had to get our best value for our buck; we had to stretch our cash and make it last. I decided it would be best if we saw the Phillies play in Pittsburgh at PNC Park in April. We could also drive instead of flying, and save a lot. The Washington Nationals were opening their brand new ballpark in April. I figured that was a no-brainer, especially since the Nats were so close. So after a few calls with Steve, Jay, and Pat, everyone seemed on board again for the season.

On April 26th, 2008 we braced ourselves for our longest road trip to date. After meal breaks and gas stops, it would be close to a six hour drive. We could have easily taken the 45-minute flight, but the goal was to keep the price down so we could attend as many games as possible this year. Pat volunteered to drive us across our own state to see the Phillies play the Pirates. He picked us all up at my house. We left around 10am and arrived in the Steel City at approximately 4pm. We checked into the Hilton Garden Inn, noticing many fans from Philadelphia had made the trip up to see a game at PNC Park. We dropped our bags and changed into our Phillies gear. We all double-checked our Phillies hats in the mirror and were on our way. The elevator, like the lobby, was packed with Phillies fans.

As we left the hotel, I noticed there were three bridges painted gold. "I heard the locals call it the Golden Triangle" Steve said. There was a small chill in the air coming off the water. We were all glad to have worn long sleeves. Before PNC Park opened in 2001, The Pirates and the Steelers both played at Three Rivers Stadium. It was named after the Allegheny, Monongahela, and Ohio rivers. As we walked across The Roberto Clemente Bridge, named after the Pirate legend, we got to see spectacular views of the ballpark. Also in the distance was Heinz Field, home of the Pittsburgh Steelers. As we approached the front of the stadium, I saw a statue of all-time great Honus Wagner. He played in Pittsburgh for the majority of his career, and in 1936 he was inducted as one of the first five players ever in Cooperstown. The Pirates staff checked our tickets and my schoolbag as we entered. Many fans passed through the turnstiles along with us, wearing Phillies and Pirates attire. The guys said, "We're starving," and Pat pointed out a concession stand right near our seats behind home plate. Pat always had the ballpark food part mapped out for us before we arrived, the same went for lunches, and dinners at restaurants. He never let us down. I could smell pizza and fried chicken in the air at the ballpark, and I couldn't wait to eat after that long drive up.

After we ate, we went to our seats in section 119 to enjoy the game. We had phenomenal views of the skyline, along with all three bridges, since there wasn't a cloud in the sky on this beautiful spring evening. We were so impressed with this stadium, which was spotless from top to bottom. It was an amazing baseball atmosphere. I remember the guys saying, "I wish they built our stadium on the water." The house was packed with both Phillies and Pirates fans in this incredible ballpark. You could hear the vendors in the background shouting, "Hot dogs here, get your hot dogs." Everyone was stuffed at that point. Another vendor cried, "Ice cold beer here, last call." We all raised our hands and grabbed a few beers before the 7th inning stretch. The Phillies would go on to beat their in-state rivals 8-6. Before I left I grabbed a postcard and a magnet, something I did at every ballpark. Pat said, "Later on we'll go out for a drink or two!"

That night we wore long sleeves again, as the weather cooled. The bar area was packed with locals and people from Philadelphia still wearing their Phillies clothing. I heard hip hop music blasting from the speakers at several of the clubs as we walked up. We enjoyed the Pittsburgh night life a little bit before heading back home the next day. We all agreed PNC Park was the nicest stadium we had seen up to that point. On the ride home we talked about Washington, which was just a few weeks away.

On Tuesday May 20th, 2008 our next game day arrived, just two weeks after Pittsburgh. We choose to go on a Tuesday, because the Phillies were in town, and we really wanted to see them at the new Nationals Park. I decided to drive and give Pat a break, since he just drove six hours each way a couple weeks before. I picked up the guys in my 1992 white Ford Explorer around 10am, and off we went to the nation's capital. During the ride down, we talked about the seven stadiums we had already seen. We still had not discussed seeing all thirty, an idea that seemed impossible. I told the guys I definitely wanted to take a picture outside the White House, and at the Washington Monument. I hadn't seen them since I was in 8th grade on a school trip, at age 13. I didn't have air conditioning in my truck, but luckily it was cool outside. We rolled the windows down on the highway and felt the strong wind hit us in the face. There was no traffic on I-95 South on that Tuesday afternoon.

We made it there in a brisk 2 hours and 20 minutes, which was nothing compared to Pittsburgh. After we parked, we strolled along to 1600 Pennsylvania Avenue to see the most famous house in America. I could see the snipers that protected the White House walking across the rooftop. The landscaping was flawless surrounding the President's home. I thought about all the history, and about previous presidents that had lived there. Many tourists snapped pictures outside, hoping to catch a glimpse of President Bush. We walked just a few more blocks down to the Lincoln Memorial, where we sat on the steps with a great view of the

Washington Monument and the Capitol building. The sun partially fought through the clouds, reflecting off the water beneath the Monument. Ducks swam across as amateur photographers took pictures. So much history happened there, from Martin Luther King's 'I have a dream' speech to Presidential Inaugurations, I thought. Steve and I enjoyed history, and all types of museums. Once we had finished doing all of our touristy things, we headed a few miles down to Nationals Park.

The National's Park had just opened the prior month and I was excited to see it. In 2007, we had flirted with the idea of seeing a game at RFK stadium, named after President John F. Kennedy's brother Robert, but we had decided to hold off and wait for this one. It was a little cooler around game time as the sun went down, but luckily we had dressed appropriately. We parked outside and entered. Everyone said, "Let's grab some food before we go to the seats." Pat said, "The Red Porch in center field is supposed to be good." I asked what kind of food they had. He replied, "Burgers, steaks, hot dogs, and fries!" One and all said, "That will work!" The restaurant was packed with both Phillies and Nationals fans who were enjoying a nice meal before the game. We heard the stadium announcer say, "Welcome to the brand new home of the Washington Nationals." We chowed down on our food like we'd never eaten before and then found our seats in right field.

During the game we took a picture with the Nationals' mascots, The Presidents. There was George Washington, Abraham Lincoln, Teddy Roosevelt, and Thomas Jefferson, all whom are on Mount Rushmore. The mascots race each other before the bottom of the fourth inning on the field. It's good entertainment for the fans. The Nationals had a state-of-the-art HD scoreboard in right field, the biggest in the League. Pat said, "I heard the Phillies are getting one just like that." It was getting chillier as the late innings approached, and some fans started to head toward the exit. We stayed until the end to see the fighting Phil's. The Phillies would go on to beat the Nationals 1-0 in an early division game in May. We took our traditional group photo together behind the National's dugout as fans exited the stadium. A player threw a ball up to us while he was leaving the field, which Jay caught. It give me a nostalgic feeling of being a kid at The Vet. On the way home my truck started to have problems. The engine light came on, and it was making some weird sounds. The lights were flickering as my battery light also lit up. It was a little scary at first, but we eventually made it home around midnight. I told Pat, "You're driving next time!" He laughed and said, "You need a new car." That wouldn't be the first time we had car trouble on a road trip. Other than that it was another successful stadium day. At this point I didn't have anything else planned, so it was back to the drawing board to find some more.

Immediately after the D.C. trip, I searched many teams and different weekends for a potential match. Only one made sense, and that was Busch Stadium in St. Louis. As a bonus, the Phillies were playing the Cardinals. Before calling all of the guys, I played around with flights, hotels, and dates. Boston & Pittsburgh were the only places we had stayed over a night, and it was a blast. Just for fun, I priced St. Louis for two nights, and to my surprise it was the exact same price as one night. I literally yelled at my computer in excitement. I texted Steve, "Call me." My phone rang within thirty seconds, and I told him the amazing news. He couldn't believe it. He said, "Call everyone up, and book it! It's my birthday weekend on top of it." I called Jay and he said, "Yeah, I'm in 100%." I called Pat, and then that's when my vibe was taken down a notch. Unfortunately, he had prior work obligations that weekend. I was crushed; I felt like Mike Tyson had punched me in the stomach. After further discussion, Pat said, "Just do it, and I'll make it up at another time." For the first time we faced a little adversity. We really didn't want to do it without him, but it was a too amazing of a deal to pass up.

So on June 14th, 2008 we traveled to St. Louis to see the Phillies play at the new Busch Stadium. We were down a man, and it didn't feel right, but we still had a game to see. We invited a friend from the neighborhood named Joey Bronico to come with us. We were happy to have another person to enjoy this adventure with us. Joey was a huge sports fan, who had a playful personality and also laughed a lot. I figured he would be a good fit with us. We arrived around 5pm on a Saturday night in the Midwest. We were all starving, so Steve suggested "The Hill". He said, "It was an Italian area in St. Louis where Yankees great Yogi Berra grew up." Jay, Joey and I all agreed to go. The majority of the population of The Hill is Italian-American and it is home to many Italian businesses and restaurants. Its name was derived from its proximity to the highest point in the city, formerly known as St. Louis Hill, which is a few blocks south at the intersection of Arsenal Street and Sublette Avenue. It was a short cab ride from downtown.

We felt very at home in this quiet Italian neighborhood. Joey said, "This reminds me of South Philly so much." Many row homes filled the streets, as kids played in the vicinity. Neighbors sat on their steps, smoking cigarettes as they watched their children roam the neighborhood with their friends. We approached a fancy restaurant, and I read the menu in the window of "Giovanni's On The Hill". I turned to everyone and said, "Looks good to me!" We ventured inside to have a very satisfying Italian dinner on this cool summer night in Missouri. Soft music played through the speakers as we ate our salads, and we anxiously awaited our entrees. Moments later, our waiter filled the table with lasagna, pasta and chicken parmesan. We didn't speak for 10 minutes, as we chewed rapidly. We finished our amazing dinner on our first trip west of the Mississippi. Joey suggested grabbing a few beers and relaxing downtown before heading back to the hotel, to which we all happily agreed.

Later that night we had some refreshing cold drinks on the strip in Old St. Louis. Cobblestones covered the streets, keeping the 1900's feel very alive. Steve said, "This reminds me of 4th and Market back home." Taxis dropped people off our age who were all dressed-up outside the bar area. Men's colognes and women's perfumes filled the air. Music from the bars could be heard from the streets. Women's high heels clicked on the sidewalks as they approached their bar of choice. We decided to call it a night around 1am. On our way back to the hotel we could see the moonlight shining brightly off the Gateway Arch, hovering over the city. The guys said, "We'll check that out tomorrow."

On Sunday morning the weather was beautiful. People walked the streets and enjoyed that summer day. Locals walked their dogs by our hotel while sipping on some fresh coffee. The Midwest sun beamed off our skins, as we walked to new Busch Stadium. Jay said, "I think we might need sunscreen." We all laughed.

Busch Stadium was home to one of the greatest players in the game, slugging first baseman Albert Pujols. We approached 700 Clark Avenue around 1pm Central Time. Just across the street the old Busch Stadium once stood. Some of the dust and debris were still visible from the old landmark, which was imploded in 2005. We were hoping for a Phillies victory, in what had been a streaky season so far for the current NL East Champs. We walked around the concourse for a while, and eventually found our seats in section 446 of the upper deck. Jay said, "I'm gonna get a nose bleed up here." I replied sarcastically, "Well I have a box of tissues for you if you need them." We posed for a great picture, with the Gateway Arch in the background. I asked Joey if he was having fun. He said, "Yes Stephen, thanks for inviting me." In the distance I could see the right field scoreboard, bearing a sign that said "2006 World Champions." I told the guys, I want to be World Champions one day. They all agreed and said, "Maybe one day." The scent of ballpark food caught our attention as we walked around. I stopped at a concession stand and grabbed a quick hot dog with mustard. The concourse was packed with fans wearing red, mainly Cardinals fans. The Phillies went back and forth with their NL Central opponent. The Phillies eventually lost that game on a late inning error by relief pitcher Flash Gordon. The guys suggested we go to see the Gateway Arch just a few blocks away.

Steve, Jay and Joey wanted to visit the Gateway Arch. Though usually I'm all for the history lesson, I wasn't feeling well after lunch at the park. The guys eventually convinced me to go. I was actually happy once inside, because I saw breathtaking views of the city and of the stadium from 630 feet above. We took the tiny claustrophobic elevator back to the ground, then walked around a little more before stopping for dinner. We enjoyed our second night in "The Lou", as locals called it. The fans in St. Louis are known as the friendliest, as Philadelphians are known as the most passionate. St. Louis' all-time great player Stan "the man" Musial is the Major League baseball logo. Steve said, "It was a great trip, and a good birthday weekend." We packed up the trunk of our cab and headed to Lambert airport.

Later that week, back in Philly, I decided we had to do one more trip in 2008. It was tougher, because a lot of us had family vacations already planned for the summer. I searched some things on the computer and saw that it was pretty reasonable to fly to Tampa Bay. I checked the Rays' schedule and found a weekend that they were home, then crunched the numbers, and realized that this was our best choice. I made my usual phone calls to Steve, Pat, and Jay. Everyone said, "Florida for the weekend? Of course we're in!" This was going to be our 10th stadium trip. I thought, "Wow! We're one-third of the way finished."

On July 30th, 2008 we all flew down to Tampa Bay. The Phillies weren't playing, so we purchased Rays hats. It was like 2007 all over again. It was nice having everyone together once more, since Pat couldn't make it to St. Louis the month before. Once we arrived, we checked into the Doubletree hotel and went straight for the pool. The palm trees swayed in the light wind, surrounding the eight-foot-deep pool. The water felt great on our hot bodies. I remember looking up, and not seeing a cloud for miles. It was such a great atmosphere; Florida just feels like baseball. A waitress came up to us and got us some drinks right there. Pat said, "This is the life." Jay said, "Charge it to the room, it's on Stephen." I shouted, "Hell no!" Jay loved to break my balls.

Later in the day we took a cab down to Tropicana Field, located in nearby Saint Petersburg. My Rays hat was drenched from the ride over. My skin was on fire from sitting by the pool. When we walked in I said, "What is that feeling? Is that air conditioning?" Steve said, "It sure is." I liked this place already! I also remember hearing the echoes from the ball off the bat throughtout the stadium, enhanced by the dome. The Rays fans were known for using cowbells at the games. At times the stadium was really loud, despite the low attendance. I thought this team could be tough to beat here, with this noise, come playoff time. In right field there was a huge sting ray tank, which fans enjoyed during the game. The ballpark was very fan-friendly, and there were lots of things to do for the kids. After we ate, we grabbed some ice cream and went down low to take a group photo. Little did we know that the Phillies and the Rays would see each other again just three months from then. Pat said, "I can't wait for the beach tomorrow."

The next afternoon we enjoyed the blazing Florida sun some more. Our skin was red and clammy as we walked along the St. Pete beach. The hot sand stuck between our toes as our feet dug in it. My

Jordan flip flops were covered in sand. The strong breeze off the ocean felt amazing, cooling us off temporarily. There was a sign that said to beware of stingrays near the ocean. I said, "I'm not going in that water." Pat said, "Man up." We eventually pool-hopped from one to another, feeling like kids down at the Jersey shore. It was another amazing trip. I remember Jay joking, saying, "10 down! 20 to go!" At this point none of us really realized we might do all thirty anyway. We were just enjoying ourselves on vacations. The Phillies played a great second half of baseball down the stretch, and found themselves ready to clinch another National League East title.

80-08 Destiny!

On September 27th, 2008, my 24th birthday, the Philadelphia Phillies clinched their second straight National League East title. Jay, Steve, and I were in attendance, as Brad Lidge remained perfect in save opportunities going 41 of 41 on the season. A few days later the Phillies hosted the Milwaukee Brewers in the National League Divisional Series. We would go on to defeat the "Brew Crew" 3 games to 1. Shane Victorino would hit a big grand slam off Brewers ace CC Sabathia in the first game of the series, which really set the tone. Next up in the National League Championship Series were the Los Angeles Dodgers. It was a hard-fought series, but the big blow came from an unexpected hero, Matt Stairs. He was signed in late

August, and was just playoff eligible. Matt hit a long home run at Dodger Stadium that propelled the Phillies into the World Series with a 4-1 NLCS victory.

The Phillies returned to the Fall Classic for the first time since 1993. Their opponent were the young and well-coached Tampa Bay Rays. The Phillies stole Game 1 on the road at Tropicana field. Ironically, we had visited that park in July. The Rays won Game 2 at home, bringing the series back to Philly, tied 1-1. The Phillies had three straight home games, and had no intention of going back to St. Petersburg.

Citizens Bank Park was rocking, and hungry for a title. The rally towels were out in full force as 45,000 fans cheered the home team to victory. The Phillies won a tight Game 3, giving us a 2 games to 1 lead. After a Phillies whopping in Game 4, which saw pitcher Joe Blanton homer in, the Phillies were on the verge of their second title in franchise history, and their first since 1980. I remember talking to the guys during every game, saying, "Can you believe this? It's finally our time!"

Game 5 had more drama then any of us had hoped for. After sloppy weather all game, the umpires decided to suspend it until further notice, with the score tied at 2 all. At that point we thought we were done. The baseball gods didn't want us to win. A few days later the game was resumed at the top of the sixth inning. The Phillies took the lead first at 3-2, only for the Rays to tie it in the next inning. Finally the Phillies took the lead at 4-3, with one thing in mind. Get the ball to Brad Lidge. The closer was 41 of 41 in the regular season, and 6 of 6 in the playoffs up until that point.

It was top of the 9th with two outs, and I'll never forget the call. Harry Kalas yelled, "The 0-2 pitch, swing and a miss, struck' em out, the Philadelphia Phillies are the 2008 World Champions of baseball!!!"

The city erupted, and Broad Street was flooded with fans from all over Philadelphia. It was the Phillies first Championship since 1980. That team included some legendary players such as Steve Carlton, Larry Bowa, Tug Mcgraw, Pete Rose, and Mike Schmidt. Later on in the night, I met the guys on Broad Street outside Methodist Hospital. People were jumping up and down. Horns were beeping as the city celebrated. We couldn't believe it, we were in shock. We were World Champions, something we never thought we would see in our lifetimes. Steve, Jay, Pat, and I all met on Halloween day for the parade. The weather was incredible for our first parade in 25 years in Philadelphia. The 76ers were the last team to win it all in 1983. An estimated two million people showed up to watch the parade on famous Broad Street. Jimmy Rollins, Chase Utley, Ryan Howard, Cole Hamels, Shane Victorino, Brad Lidge, Carlos Ruiz, Pat Burrell and the rest of the 2008 Philadelphia Phillies were World Series Champions. I'll never forget it for the rest of my life. We all said it was 80-08 destiny!

PNC Park in Pittsburgh

Jay, Pat, Me and Steve at PNC Park

National's Park in Washington, DC

HD Scoreboard at National's Park

The White House

Lincoln Memorial

Jay, Steve, Joey & Me at Busch Stadium in St. Louis

Busch Stadium from the top of the Gateway Arch

The Hill in St. Louis

The Gateway Arch in St. Louis

The Front of Tropicana Field in Tampa Bay, FL

Tropicana Field- Home of the Rays

Jay, Pat, Steve and Me at Tropicana Field

The pool at the hotel in Tampa Bay

Me at the 2008 Championship Parade on Broad Street

World Series Float on Broad Street in South Philly

Race to the Repeat

The Phillies are the Champions of baseball. The city was buzzing off of that for a couple of months into the winter. Everything in the stores was Phillies World Series clothing and memorabilia. Opening day 2009 couldn't come fast enough. I had a busy year of planning trips ahead of me. We would have an extra swagger to us this year as champions. The Phillies schedule came out, and I didn't know where to start. My mind was racing with so many thoughts and different scenarios. My preliminary itinerary was as follows: Miami in April to see the Phillies vs Marlins, in May double dip in New York and see the Mets and Yankees play the Phillies in their brand new ballparks, in June head down to Texas and see the Houston Astros, and in July see the San

Diego Padres at Petco Park. Our first trip out west, and in California! This was a lot to digest, so after speaking with everyone it was a go. I charged all these trips on my credit card and we paid it off throughout the winter months. I was happy with being at 13 stadiums by this year's end.

When opening day rolled around, we were extra excited to see the Phillies get their championship rings. The 2008 season was an amazing ride for them, and for us, something we would never forget for the rest of our lives. We prepared for South Beach in Miami, Florida. This was my first time in Miami. The guys had visited there last summer, but not for baseball. I was looking forward to getting a tan, drinking some cold beers on the beach, and seeing another stadium.

On April 13, 2009 the Phillies' longtime announcer and beloved icon Harry Kalas died. He collapsed in the broadcasters' booth just before the game was set to start in Washington. His legendary voice called many classic Phillies games since 1971, including the 1980 and 2008 World Series championships. I met him many times as a kid, in the Veterans Stadium parking lot before games. He was always friendly and signed autographs for everyone. The Phillies would wear an HK patch for the entire 2009 season, in his honor. His incredible voice and passion for the game would be missed dearly. He died doing what he loved. The Phillies booth would never be the same again. He passed at age 73, and is in the Baseball Hall of Fame as a broadcaster. I'll never forget Harry saying, "That ball is outta here, Michael Jack Schmidt."

On April 27th our flight landed in sunny Miami, Florida. There were palm trees and girls in bikinis everywhere. We rented a brand-new condo at 10th & Ocean Drive, which was in the heart of all the action. Ocean Drive is the strip of Miami Beach with so many restaurants, shops, and bars, facing the wide beach and the ocean. We all bought some 190 octanes from Fat Tuesday and headed across the street to the beach. Baseball is our first love, but there's nothing wrong with relaxing in the hot Florida sun once in a while. The breeze off the ocean felt great, considering it was in the 80's all afternoon. We took a dip in the aqua blue waters of Miami several times to cool off. Women tanned topless on Miami Beach, just feet away from us. After soaking up some sun rays, and having a little buzz from the adult beverages, we planned for the night. Pat found us a nice Italian place to eat at right around the corner. Pat said to me, "Don't worry, they have chicken parm." He knew that's all I ate. There was a variety of things to choose from, as we listened to Frank Sinatra through the speakers. Nothing like "Old Blue Eyes" while you eat. The food was great. Pat said, "Ocean Drive time!"

Later on we tried a few bars and clubs on Ocean Drive. Mango's was packed with people, still in their bathing suits. Dancers provided entertainment to the beat of the house music playing. All different types of people walked the streets of Miami, from all walks of life. People lined up outside Fat Tuesday, which was right below our condo. I said, "Everyone loves those 190 Octanes." We were exhausted from the flight in, the beach and all of the partying. We called it a night around 2am.

The Miami sun shone through our condo windows and woke us up around 9am. We threw on our swim trunks and tank tops, then proceeded to a great breakfast spot on Collins Ave. The aroma of eggs, sauage, and fresh coffee filled the diner as we entered. Many people were dressed in their beach attire, as we were. We ate the most important meal of the day, and off we went to the beach. People boogie-boarded on the waves of the ocean as we sipped our Coronas. Lifeguards blew their whistles a few times at some aggressive swimmers. Guys and girls rode wave runners on the clear blue waters of Miami all day. The guys had their headphones on, and sucked up the Flordia sun for the rest of the afternoon. The day zipped by and it was almost time for the game.

Dolphin Stadium, now known as Sun Life Stadium, was home to the Marlins and the Miami Dolphins. It has hosted many Super Bowls over the years. The stadium opened in the late 80's, and the Marlins were set to get a new ballpark in 2012. There weren't many people at the game. The Marlins didn't draw well, despite two World Series titles since 1997. The upper deck was completely empty, which gave me a nostalgic feeling of The Vet in the 90's. Dolphin Stadium is one of the few stadiums left that still host football and baseball. We didn't bother going to our assigned seats; we just snuck down behind home plate. There was no dome on this ballpark, unlike Tropicana Field in Tampa Bay, so we were sweating badly. Our bodies were beat red from the beach all day. We were badly dehydrated from all the drinking and the sun. The air was sticky and humid around game time. We all ran to the concessions and grabbed a few bottles of cold water. Pat had reservations for a late dinner, so we didn't eat at the game. The Phillies trailed all game after starting pitcher Brett Myers gave up a three run homerun in the first inning. The Phillies ended up coming back and winning this game on a clutch grand slam by center fielder Shane Victorino in the 9th inning. We all cheered in excitement as our defending champion Phillies won this thriller. Pat said, "Let's grab dinner, then we'll go to Nikki Beach on Front & Ocean." We took it easy on our final night in South Beach. We hung out at Nikki Beach. It's a popular club that sits on the beach itself. The line was long to get in, since everyone had the same idea as us. Music blasted from inside; we were eager to get in. The bouncer asked for our ID's and said, "It's a twenty dollar cover charge for guys." We relaxed in lounge chairs and drank beers as the ocean breeze hit us one final time. I said, "I love Miami!" The guys all agreed. We didn't have to wait long to get back on the road once we got home. Our first New York trip of the month, to brand new Citi Field, was creeping up in just a few weeks.

On Thursday May 7th we jumped on NJ Transit and headed back to the Big Apple. It felt like 2007 again, the guys said. We took the Long Island Railroad into Flushings, NY. The train was packed with Mets fans excited to see the brand new Citi Field. We knew the environment was going to be hostile. We all said we were division rivals on the road, not to mention defending World Champions, and agreed to talk trash back to the Mets fans, but to keep it friendly and respectful. Mr. Met, the mascot, was outside waiving to fans as they arrived. As we approached Citi Field I couldn't help but think it resembled Ebbets Field, the former home of the Brooklyn Dodgers. We took the escalator up through the Jackie Robinson rotunda to our seats. Jackie Robinson broke baseball's color barrier back on April

15th, 1947. We thought the stadium was nice, but not nicer than Citizens Bank Park. As I looked around, I saw a lot of Phillies fans who had made the trip up from Philly. It made us not the only enemies here tonight, though we had our 2008 World Series shirts on and I'm sure some fans didn't like that. Some Mets fans called us chumps, and I remember responding with, "You mean champs!" Everyone laughed at that.

We walked around a little and checked out the rest of Citi Field. One cool thing I noticed was that they brought over the old home run apple from Shea Stadium. It went off every time a Mets player hit a home run in old Shea. The concourse was packed with people wearing David Wright t-shirts and jerseys. He's one of the best third basemen in the league. The stadium was huge and seemed hard to hit home runs in, the fences were so deep in the outfield. We found our seats in the upper deck, and we had a clear view of the Pepsi Porch, in right field. Smoke from the concessions could be seen in the air, as food was being made for the large crowd on hand. The smell of fresh peanuts, and ballpark franks caught my nose. I took my camera out and snapped many photos of Citi Field. Our overall experience was a fun night. The Phillies lost that game, but that didn't mess up our night. We just loved coming to New York. We took the Long Island Railroad back into Penn Station. Fans heckled us, and told us to go back to Philly. We didn't let it get to us, as it's part of the game. We were the champions, and we expected this on every road trip this year. We would see New York again very soon.

Growing up I always dreamed of seeing the Phillies play at Yankee Stadium. Secretly the Yankees were my second favorite team. On May 23rd, I finally got to see that match-up. We jumped on the NJ transit once again. By now I swore I took that train more than I drove my own car. The ride was a little bumpy, and the train as always was filled with people heading to New York for both business and pleasure. Once we arrived at Penn Station, we walked down a few blocks to D Train subway. As we arrived at 161st street in the Bronx, we could see the old Yankee Stadium that stood across the street. It was set for demolition soon, and we were glad we could see it one more time. Sometimes I wish they would have kept it open as a museum; it was one of a kind. The new stadium looked like a Coliseum. Jay and I snapped many photos of the exterior. Lines of people formed outside, waiting to get in on this wonderful Saturday afternoon in New York. Vendors yelled "Get your programs here!" Many ticket scalpers asked us if we needed tickets for the game. We just ignored them and headed to the gate. We broke Steve's chops that afternoon, because his ticket wouldn't scan, and the worker was giving him a hard time about it. We said, "Put it through the scanner buddy." That was the running joke of the day.

Once inside I ran behind home plate to take a quick picture, but a guard yelled at me, saying, "Go to your correct seats" in his thick New York accent. I said, "Give me a break; it's a picture." We did, however, find our correct seats in the upper deck. The ballpark resembled old Yankee Stadium a bit however, this was brand new with a large concourse. We proudly wore our Phillies gear at every road game that year. Steve said, "This is great! The Phillies are at Yankee Stadium as World Champs!" We all were just as excited as Steve.

It was a comfortable afternoon, with a nice breeze, on that Memorial Day weekend. We were enjoying baseball on the greatest stage in sports. This stadium wasn't as historical as the old ballpark was, but in time it would be. I thought, a new stadium, and new memories... I remember saying, "This could be a World Series preview." In centerfield the Yankees had a museum with autographed baseballs from every player who ever played for them. I thought that was amazing. Phillies rookie John Mayberry, Jr. would hit his first career homerun in this game. His father acutally played for the Yankees back in the day. The Phillies lost that game in the bottom of the 9th. Alex Rodriguez hit a walk off home run against Brad Lidge, blowing the save. This was something he would do a lot of in 2009, after having that magical perfect season just the year before. The Phillies would take two out of three games from the Yanks that weekend, but they could have easily swept them out of the Bronx. This was a true measuring stick for our team going forward. The same as Citi Field, fans broke our stones on the train back. We ignored them and focused on Texas, which was our next trip.

Only a few short weeks later, we were getting ready to make our first trip down south to Texas. We landed in Houston on the weekend of June 6th. As we searched for a taxi, the Texas heat hit us like a ton of bricks. I instantly had to lift my Astros hat up and wipe the sweat off my head. After checking into the Doubletree hotel, we wandered downtown for a while. We liked to observe how other people live in different cities. In the distance we saw the Toyota Center, home to the Houston Rockets. I joked with the guys, saying,

"Let's try and play a game of basketball inside." Everyone laughed, and said, "You're crazy." Jay said, "Remember I got kicked out of Soldier Field in Chicago." However, we did find a basketball court shortly after that. We shot some hoops in the 95 degree Texas sun. Our skin was red and we were exhausted after just 15 minutes. My t-shirt was drenched in perspiration. Steve said, "I'm dying of dehydration! I need a Gatorade." I told the guys we should hang at the hotel and get ready for dinner. Luckily we had a pool there to cool off in. We found a nice southern bar later that night. The people were all friendly and welcoming. Jay bought the first round of beers for everyone. He said, "To Houston, boys." We loved to enjoy the nightlife in other cities, along with restaurants and baseball. We called it a night not too long after midnight. The next day we got ready to see Minute Maid Park.

The home of the Houston Astros was opened in 2000. This was the second stadium we had visited with a dome, and I was looking forward to the air conditioning. The guys said, "This Texas heat is killing us!" I agreed with them. We walked on Crawford Avenue and entered through the right field gate. When we got to our seats, we talked about the Astro teams of the 90's, about greats like Jeff Bagwell and Craig Biggio. They were known as the Killer Bees. The Astros were in rebuilding mode at this time, with former Phillies GM Ed Wade in charge. As Phillies fans from the 90's, we knew all too well about rebuilding. It was a chill atmosphere on this Sunday afternoon in June. The stadium was half full on this steaming day in Texas. We noticed that they had a train in center field. I asked one of the fans what that was for, and she responded, "Every time an Astro player hits a home run, it moves across the tracks." We nodded.

"Also, in center field, they have something called Tal's hill. Tal's hill is a tribute to old Crosley field in Cincinnati. Most players hate it, because you're running slightly up a hill to catch a fly ball. It could cause serious injury." After a lap around the stadium, we stopped at the team store to purchase some souvenirs. I grabbed a couple of postcards, while Pat grabbed a shot glass. Jay said, "This might be one of my favorite stadiums." The guys said, "Houston was fun; let's get ready for Cali baby next month!"

Our most anticipated trip of the year had arrived. We were heading to San Diego, California. When I pictured California in my head, I could see guys surfing waves and girls lying out on the beach. I could picture those same girls walking around in bikinis and people in convertibles with the top down. On July 3th we prepared for our six-hour flight. Pat and I put our Bose headsets on and relaxed all the way over. All I could think about was the beach and the Pacific Ocean. Jay also listened to music on his iPod, while Steve read a book. The stewardess asked us several times if we needed anything, but we were ok. The flight zipped by, and when the pilot said, "flight attendants brace for landing," our smiles grew larger.

As the plane was coming up to the gate, I started chatting with a guy next to me. He said, "Are you from Philly?" He saw I had my Phillies hat on. I said, "Yeah, me and my three friends are here to see Petco Park." He responded, "That's good, you'll like it." I said, "This will be our 13th stadium we've seen in the league; we're trying to see all 30." He smiled at me and said, "That's great! I've seen 20 myself." My mouth dropped. I said, "20? Wow that's amazing." He said,

"While you're here you guys should check out the Angels Stadium too; it's only an hour and a half train ride from here." That's when everything changed.

I flipped on my phone and checked the Angels schedule. I said to the guys, "If they are home this weekend, then it's destiny for us to do all 30." The results on my phone came back and I said, "You're kidding me, they're home!" I couldn't believe that we would see two stadiums that weekend. We would be at 14 different ones, almost half way done. I asked the guys if they were okay with going to Anaheim on Sunday. They all instantly said, "Hell yeah!" That was the first moment when I knew we would do all 30 ballparks. We grabbed our heavy luggage from the overhead compartment and patiently waited to exit the plane. Steve turned to me and said, "Two for the price of one." I said, "I know! This is nuts." We were so excited from this great news that we almost forgot that we were in San Diego. Shortly after we checked into our hotel, called Porto Vista, in the downtown area. Pat said, "Let's go to Mission Beach, it's a 10 minute cab ride from here." We all agreed, and went.

Mission Beach had many locals and tourists on it. It was nice to see the mountains in the background. I said, "This is different, this is Cali!" Pat said, "I wonder if the Pacific Ocean is as blue as it is in my dreams." We all laughed. The sand felt so soft and warm under our feet, as the cool breeze off the ocean was just right. The beer tasted extra cold as we didn't have a care in the world. After enjoying the Southern California sun for a few hours, we headed back to get showers. Pat said, "We would grab dinner in Little Italy around the corner, and then head over to the Gaslamp Quarter." The Gaslamp had many bars, clubs, and restaurants for people our age. That sounded great to me. I remember partying on a rooftop bar that had a view of Petco Park. I said to Pat, "Tomorrow we will be there!" Then Steve said, "On Sunday we'll be in Anaheim." Cigar smoke filled the room as we enjoyed this amazing night in San Diego. This was shaping up to be our best baseball weekend yet.

The next day, July 4th, we headed over to Petco Park. The Padres were playing the Los Angeles Dodgers. The weather was just right, a cool 70 degrees at game time. A cool breeze was coming off the San Diego bay. As we approached the stadium, I saw an advertisement for Comic Con. Many celebrities and television personalities would attend. Most fans would dress up in their favorite Star Wars or super hero movie costumes. "I've been dying to go!" I said. The guys knew I was a huge horror and comic book geek. The enormous Convention Center could be seen in the distance.

We arrived at Petco Park, and saw all the palm trees swaying in the breeze. I saw the Tony Gwynn statue outside. Tony Gywnn was one of the greatest Padres ever and is in the Baseball Hall of Fame. He was nicknamed "Mr Padre." He had a career batting average of .338 and spent 20 years with the ballclub. We entered Petco Park through the outfield, which was different. People laid out in the outfield on the grass; it reminded me of a spring training game. Kids roamed around the area playing, it reminded me of FDR Park back home. We found out seats and enjoyed a nice beer in sunny California. The smell of fresh food from the concessions was calling our names. Steve said, "I can't believe we're in Cailfornia." I replied, "This is incredible." The Western Metal Supply Company building could be seen in left field. Fans leaned over the balconies taking pictures. I said, "I think those tickets are expensive." The stadium was packed with both Dodgers and Padres fans on this amazing summer day. Around the 5th inning Pat said, "You guys wanna go to the beach?" We all said, "Definitely." I thought to myself how I already loved the West Coast.

On July 5th, we took the Amtrak train up to Anaheim and saw the Angels play. We saw amazing scenery along the coastline on our way up. People were surfing the waves on the Orange County beaches. The train conductor said, "Next stop Angels Stadium." We hopped up from our seats and gathered our belongings. Their stadium was a little older-looking from the outside. I took a picture of the large Angels helmets out front. I remember I made the guys buy Angels hats. I said, "Come on guys, for the picture." They all laughed, and said, "You love your damn pictures." The Angels were playing the Baltimore Orioles on this humid Sunday afternoon. We talked to some fans, who were really friendly. They asked where I was from, and I said, "Philly." I always tried to mingle with the fans at other stadiums. I always enjoyed talking baseball. We found our seats in the upper deck as we ate some lunch. I could see the Honda Center in the distance, home of the Anaheim Mighty Ducks. The guys said, " I love the Mighty Ducks movies!" We left the game around the sixth inning, and caught the train back to downtown San Diego. On the ride back I said to the guys, "14 stadiums down! We're having the time of our lives right now."

That night we had dinner in Little Italy, which was amazing. Italian flags moved in the light wind as we strolled along outside.

People of all ages and backgrounds were enjoying this phenomenal evening in the downtown area. We put on our nice button up shirts and ironed jeans, for one more night in the Gaslamp Quarter. The California atmosphere was incredible, I didn't want to go home. We had a lot of fun on that San Diego trip. Once I realized we could do two stadiums in one trip, it changed everything. All of sudden, 30 ballparks didn't seem so far away. We all agreed that this was our favorite trip to date. Steve would always refer to this trip as our double play.

We took a break for a few months after that trip. We enjoyed the summer and watched the Phillies in many prime time games. The Phillies would acquire Cleveland Indians ace Cliff Lee at the trade deadline, which shook the National League. They also signed veteran Pedro Martinez for the second half of the season. The Phillies now had Cole Hamels and Cliff Lee at the top of their rotation. They were poised for another deep October run, and the race to the repeat was on.

As August approached, I really wanted to at least try to do one more stadium trip. Steve would text me from time to time, asking, "Any new trips for us?" So he motivated me to squeeze another one in. California wasn't cheap, so I wanted to give the guys some room to recoup. The Phillies had made a blockbuster deal; now it was my turn to pull something off. I kept eyeing this one game in September. The Phillies were playing in Milwaukee at Miller Park. Prices were a tad high and maybe a little out of our range just for one trip. So I started searching for multiple stadiums at once. That Padres, Angels combo just last month really changed my outlook on things. But I was drawing a blank. I remember Pat calling me up and saying, "Check Chicago, maybe we could do the White Sox, and then take a train up to Milwaukee." As requested, I searched that scenario, and to my surprise it was so much cheaper to stay in Chicago. I called everyone up and explained to them what I had in mind. Everyone loved it, and it was reasonably cheap. I was extra pumped, because we would be doing two stadiums again. This would put us at 16, three ahead of my original plan for the year. Not too long after that conversation, I booked our final trip for late September. Summer was over, and the Phillies were eyeing their third consecutive National League East crown. The weather was becoming cooler, and playoff baseball loomed. We were excited for yet another year of October baseball.

We left for Chicago on September 26, which was almost two years to the day since we were there last. This time around we walked around the downtown area called "The Loop". We stopped at Millennium Park, took some pictures of The Bean, and saw the Buckingham fountain. The fountain is featured in the hit 90's show "Married with Children". I said, "It's almost game time." We jumped in a cab and off we went to US Cellular Field, home of the White Sox. The White Sox ended their long championship drought in 2005, with their first title since 1917. Our cab dropped us off on the south side of Chicago.

The White Sox were playing the Detroit Tigers in this American League showdown. Chicago's lefty ace Mark Buehrle was on the mound. Buehrle had thrown a perfect game just two months prior.

We walked around US Cellular, formally known as Comiskey Park for a few innings, and then finally found our seats in the second level. Only Jay, Pat, and I had on brand new White Sox hats, as Steve had his hair slicked back with gel. Steve said, "Pat, you look like Easy E from the rap group NWA with that sweatshirt on." Jay and I, both busted out laughing. Steve said, "I'm only messing with ya bro." The scent of pretzels, burgers, and cotton candy filled the concourse. We walked up and down the ramps which remind me of being a kid at The Vet. The breathtaking views of the skyline and the Sears Towers were visble in the dark Chicago sky. I always enjoyed hearing longtime White Sox broadcaster Ken Harrelson call a game on tv. When a Sox player homered his catch phrase was, "You can put it on the board yessssssss!!!" Sometimes we lost interest in the games, when the Phillies didn't play. We decided we weren't going to stay the whole game. We grabbed a round of beers and talked about going to a nice club on Division Street that night. Steve said, "At least we'll see the Phillies play tomorrow in Milwaukee."

On Sunday morning we got up nice and early to catch our train to Milwaukee. It was dark and cloudy with a chance of rain. It was breezy with the temperature in the low 50's. During the ride we talked about the Phillies playoff chances and what they had to do repeat. We knew it wouldn't be easy. At one point I remember looking down at my train ticket stub that said Chicago to Milwaukee. I turned to the guys and said, "This is crazy; we've done a lot this year." We have done more traveling in a few years than some people do in their entire lives, I thought. The train was packed with many different people, heading to many different destinations. Around 11:30 am we arrived at Miller Park. The ballpark has been home to the Brew Crew since 2001. The outside of the stadium looked like something out of the future. Jay said to me, "Take a picture!" But I already had my camera out. I kept telling the guys, "I hope we get to see Bernie the Brewer slide down his slide, which he does if a Brewers player homers." Miller Park has a dome, but the roof was open that day. The weather was overcast with rain in the forecast, so we wondered if it started raining how fast they could get the roof closed. I joked with the guys and said, "We gotta drink a Miller Lite in Miller Park." After we grabbed our Miller Lite's, we found our seats behind home plate. The Phillies had a chance to clinch the division in this game, with the work horse Joe Blanton on the hill. It started to drizzle in the 5th inning, so we got to see the retractable roof in action. It only took minutes to close, not messing up the game at all. The guys said, "We need that in Philly." I agreed. I took a picture of Bernie's Dugout in left field. I wish we could have taken a picture with him. The Phillies would lose this game to the Brewers. "I guess we gotta wait one more game to wrap up NL East title." The guys said. We took the train back to Chicago later in the day. We enjoyed our final night in Chi-town, and our last stadium trip of the year. Steve said, "16 down, 14 to go."

Later that week, the Phillies clinched their third straight NL East title. They defeated the Colorado Rockies in the first round in 4 games, getting revenge on them for the 2007 playoffs, when they swept us out. It was a tough series, but the Phillies prevailed. The Phillies would host and defeat the Los Angeles Dodgers in 5 games, for the second straight year in the NLCS.

We advanced to the World Series once more, facing the New York Yankees. The race to the repeat was really on. Cliff Lee dominated Game 1 in Yankee Stadium. Chase Utley added two home runs giving us a 1-0 lead in the series and stealing home field advantage. The Yankees won the next three games, two at Citizens Bank Park, which put us in a huge hole. We won Game 5, but eventually lost the series in game 6. Our repeat hopes were dead. The Yankees won their 27th World Series championship in franchise history. We were disappointed, but really proud of our team for winning back-to-back pennants.

Phillies at Marlins – Sun Life Stadium in Miami

Jay, Pat, Steve and Me at Sun Life Stadium

Ocean Drive in South Beach

Miami Beach

Front of Citi Field in Flushing's New York

Jay, Me, Pat and Steve at Citi Field – Phillies vs Mets

Front of the New Yankee Stadium

Phillies at Yankees on Memorial Day Weekend

Minute Maid Park in Houston, TX

The Train in the outfield at Minute Maid Park

Petco Park in San Diego, CA

Me, Pat, Steve, Jay at Petco Park on July 4th Weekend

Angel Stadium in Anaheim, CA

Jay, Steve, Me and Pat at Angel Stadium

US Cellular Field

Jay, Pat, Steve and Me at US Cellular Field in Chicago

The Bean in Chicago

Buckingham Fountain in Chicago

Miller Park

Jay, Pat, Steve and Me at Miller Park in Milwaukee, WI

West Coast Swing

On December 17th, 2009 Phillies fans everywhere were outraged. Fan favorite Cliff Lee was traded to the Seattle Mariners for prospects. In a separate deal, we acquired Blue Jays ace Roy Halladay. We were happy and sad at the same time. Phillies GM Ruben Amaro said we had to replenish the farm system. We were hoping this move wouldn't hurt us come the season or the playoffs. I spoke with the guys in January of 2010, saying, "It's time to hit the West Coast." They agreed. As always, I looked at every option we had. I immediately saw that the Phillies were playing in Arizona, San Diego, Los Angeles, and finally in Atlanta. I told the guys we would start with Arizona in April, and then we would see the Colorado Rockies play at Coors Field in May. We really wanted to return to San Diego, and we lucked out with the schedule. The Phillies played at Petco on a Sunday afternoon, then at Dodger Stadium on a Monday, in August. We would end the season in Atlanta for our final weekend of the year.

We had a brutal winter in Philly, which dumped 71 inches of snow in total. April couldn't come fast enough. We were excited to see the back-to-back National League Champs on the road.

We prepared for our four-hour flight to Phoenix to see the Arizona Diamondbacks. We had our usual flight routine, with our headphones or books to help the time pass. When we got off the plane, I instantly remarked on the desert heat beating down upon us. The guys said, "I hope we have a pool?" I said, "We sure do, I made sure of that." We usually took cabs from the airport, since Uber wouldn't be around for a few more years. That's when a limo driver approached us and said, "Need a ride?" We said, "How much?" He replied, "Give me $40!" We said, "Why not, let's ride in style for once." We split it four ways, and headed to the hotel. Along the way we joked, "We've made it now." Acting like big shots in a limo. I felt like Kevin McCallister, in "Home Alone 2", when he was driving to Duncan's Toy Chest. We thanked our driver and checked in to the Hilton Garden Inn. We saw our pool from the balcony window. We said, "That looks great!" We couldn't wait to jump in. Besides having the pool, we also had a full gym with a basketball court. Me and Jay's eyes lit up, as we are huge basketball fans. Jay passed me a ball and said, "Come on, let's play a quick game or two." The ball echoed throughout the empty gym. We played a few pick-up games against Steve and Pat, but they stood no chance. After basketball, we relaxed in the pool for an hour or so, while the Phoenix sun beamed down on us. The cold water felt amazing after just sweating in the gym. Shortly after that, we got dressed in our Phillies gear and ready for Chase Field.

On the cab ride over we talked about the 2001 World Series. How a young Diamondbacks team defeated the almighty New York Yankees in game 7. The guys said, "Let's not forget they did have Curt Shilling, and Randy Johnson." I replied, "That was a great series." We got out of the cab, and saw Chase Field. An abundance of Diamondbacks fans covered the outside area surrounding the large ballpark. The roof was open on this hot day. We were hoping they would close it and put the air on. I said, "It feels like Texas out here." Pat said, "Man up! It's the desert." We all laughed. There was a feature I was really looking forward to, and that was the pool in right center field. Kids paddled back and forth while watching the game. "It was the only stadium in the league with one, but it was for private parties only." Pat said. We did offer the guard a twenty dollar bill, but he gave us a dirty look, so we moved on. After grabbing some food and a cold beer, we headed over to our seats down the third base line. I remember saying to the boys, "17 stadiums how does it feel?" They replied, "Great! I don't want it to end." The Phillies won that game on two Jayson Werth home run balls, sending us back to the hotel happy.

The next day we just relaxed by the pool again, and shot some more hoops. There wasn't much going on, so I asked the guys, "You wanna do another game? It's at 1pm." They said, "Might as well." So we went back to Chase Field for an encore. This was the first trip in which we saw two games at one stadium in the same weekend. Overall Phoenix was a fun experience, just a little hot. I said, "Luckily we had that pool at the hotel." The guys said, "Next up Coors Field."

On Saturday May 15th, we woke up to a cool spring morning in Philadelphia. I could hear the birds chirping outside, while the bright sunlight entered my bedroom. Excitement was in the air, because the summer was just around the corner. We were preparing for our weekend in the Mile High City. I finished packing up my suitcase and went outside. Pat's fiancée Jackie was driving us to the airport that morning. We loaded her trunk up and we were on our way. In the car we talked about Colorado, specifically Denver. I turned to Pat and said, "I can't wait to have a Coors Light at Coors Field." He said, "Yeah me too." As we arrived at our departing gate, we thanked Jackie for the ride. We printed our boarding passes at the kiosk, then proceeded to security. Once through, the guys grabbed some Starbucks while I had some breakfast at Mcdonalds. Our four hour flight was fairly smooth, with just a little turbulence along the way.

We arrived in the Denver area around 1pm local time. I walked off the plane in shorts and flip flops, and to my surprise it was freezing out. Luckily I'd packed warm for the weekend. We took a taxi to Hotel VQ. It reminded me a lot of the Travelodge on Penrose Avenue back in South Philly. Just next door was Invesco Field, now known as Sports Authority Field, home of the Denver Broncos since 2001. It was also referred to as the Mile High Stadium. Just in the distance Elitch Gardens Theme Park filled the sky. The huge white roller coaster was one of the main attractions, along with a water park that only opened in the summer. Kids packed the park on this chilly Saturday afternoon. After checking into the hotel, Pat said, "We should go downtown to the 16th Street Mall." We said, "Sounds good!"

The 16th Street Mall was a popular tourist attraction. It was an outdoor mall with many shops, restaurants, and even a bowling alley. Bright green trees filled the sidewalks, as people relaxed on the wooden benches reading books. Teenagers rode their skateboards over the cobblestone streets, as mothers pushed baby strollers around. A bus provided pedestrians with free rides up and down the strip, as they held their heavy shopping bags. Pat suggested Smashburger for lunch. The menu consisted of burgers, chicken sandwiches, and salads. The smell of fried food filled the air, while rock music played throughout the speakers. We checked out some souvenir shops along the way, before I told the guys, "It's almost game time; we probably should get ready soon." Jay flagged down a taxi and we were on our way to Coors Field.

After a ten minute ride we arrived at Coors Field. It was a chilly May night, so we wore our sweatshirts and hoodies to the game. I had my Phillies hat on even though they weren't playing. I snapped a picture of the beautiful exterior, then we went inside. The Rockies were playing the Washington Nationals that day. It's been home to the Rockies since 1995, their expansion year. I was telling the guys, "I remember those great Rockies players of the 90's. Larry Walker, Vinny Castilla, and Dante Bichette." Jay and Steve said, "They used to kill the Phillies." Denver is also known as the Mile High City, because it sits a mile above sea level. In the upper deck there is a row of purple seats to mark 5,280 feet above sea level exactly. In Coors

Field the balls fly out of the park faster than at others because of the thin air. I said, "You could always see a crooked number here on the scoreboard." The guys said, "It's definitely not a pitchers park!"

We walked around a bit, then proceeded to our seats. Pat said, "How about that Coors Light?" I said, "Of Course! "It'll taste better here." The Phillies weren't playing in this game so our interest in the outcome was minimal. We noticed the concourse had batting cages so we decided to take a few swings. It reminded me of Veterans Stadium a lot. We would always do that back home when we were kids. Funny story was, I remember when Steve accidentally hit my brother Mark in the head with a bat at the batting cages at The Vet. He got stitches at the first aid center, but pulled through all right. The Rocky Mountains were visible from the upper deck seats, covered in snow. I took a few pictures of the fountains in center field and then we headed to the exit gates. The Rockies beat the National's 4-3.

Later that night, back at the hotel, we had dinner at our rooftop restaurant. Music was playing throughout, as the smell of steak was everywhere. Most of downtown Denver was visible. We could see the Pepsi Center in the distance, home to the Denver Nuggets since 1999. We asked the bartender to put ESPN on, because the Philadelphia Flyers were in the Stanley Cup Finals. Their opponent was the Chicago Blackhawks. The Flyers won that game, but eventually lost the series to the Blackhawks, 4 games to 2. We had a few more rounds of beer after dinner, and then decided to wrap up our Denver trip and call it a night. We had an early flight to catch in the morning from Denver International Airport. I said, "18 stadiums! Another one under the belt."

On May 29th, Roy Halladay threw a perfect game against the Florida Marlins at Sun Life Stadium. It was the twentieth perfect game in Major League history and just the second in Phillies history. The week prior I had had knee surgery but I remember running up the steps in excitement anyway. I called Steve up and yelled, "Perfect game!!" He said, "This is great!" That wouldn't be the last time that season that Roy Halladay did something special. It was the first time a Phillies pitcher threw a perfect game, since Jim Bunning on June 21st, 1964 at Shea Stadium.

It was early June, and the weather was finally warming up. Kids were finishing up school for the year, and families were heading down to the shore for summer vacation. Our next trip wasn't until the end of August, but I was itching to do another one. For fun I started looking up some trips for July. We had wanted to visit Cleveland for a while now. I also started checking the Detroit Tigers' schedule; I was trying to pull off the two at once. I found this one weekend where both teams were playing at home. I knew the cities were less than two hours apart from each other. I realized that if we could pull this off, we would be at 22 stadiums by the end of the year. After searching for a while, I came up with a plan. It wouldn't be easy, and I was wondering if the guys would be on board for my wild pitch. I called Steve up and said, "I have a crazy idea." He asked, "What do ya got?" I responded, "Cleveland and Detroit in July!" He said, "Seriously?" I said, "We would fly out of BWI in Baltimore to Cleveland. We catch a game in Progressive field, and then the next day we take a greyhound bus up to Detroit, and see a game at Comerica Park. After we're finished there, we'll fly from Detroit back to Baltimore, then drive home." He said, "You're crazy man." I said,

"It will save us a lot of money, and we'll knock out two more stadiums." He replied, "If everyone's in, then I am." I spoke with the other guys and, after some convincing, we had another trip planned. Flying out of BWI was half the price of Philadelphia International Airport.

July 24th approached quickly. I told the guys we would have to pack light because we wouldn't be able to bring large bags in to the game in Detroit. I said, "Squeeze everything into a school bag, to play it safe." We decided it was easier to sleep in Baltimore the night before. Pat drove us down again. I said, "It feels like 07 again." Our flight was 8am on Saturday morning, and we wanted to make sure we had enough time. I was a little worried at first, because this trip was complicated. If we missed that bus on Sunday morning in Detroit then this whole trip was a bust. I tried to relax and enjoy Cleveland first. The weather was lousy with a light drizzle in the air, but nothing to postpone the game. First thing on the list before the game was the Rock and Roll Hall of Fame. We weren't huge fans of the genre, but we were still interested in seeing it. Pat said, "Just add this to our resume." As we walked up it resembled a glass pyramid. Many decades of legendary musicians' work was inside. It was downtown on Lake Erie. The Hall of Fame is located in Cleveland because a local DJ named Alan Freed coined the phrase "Rock and Roll." We walked around a bit and saw a nice display of the Beatles, one of the greatest groups to ever do it. Down the hall we saw some more displays of the late greats Prince, James Brown, Ray Charles, and Michael Jackson. We walked around some more and then I saw the king, Elvis Presley. I said, "Thank you, thank you very much." The guys said, "I think it's time for the game." I laughed.

Progressive Field, formerly known as Jacobs Field, has been home to the Cleveland Indians since 1994. Locals call the park "The Jake". The Indians had a sellout streak of 455 straight games between the years 1995-2001. They had the tarp on the field due to the rain all day, but the sun was sneaking through the clouds around first pitch. The Indians were playing the AL East Tampa Bay Rays. Pat said, "We'll grab a few beers here but after the game we'll eat at Lounge 21 just a few blocks away." I joked and asked, "Do you have to be 21 to get in?" Pat smirked and said, "No." We made a few laps around the concourse and eventually found our seats. We had a great view of the Cleveland skyline as we savored our ice cold beers. Heritage Park, which was the Indians Hall of Fame could be seen in center field. I told the guys, "I remember watching Sandy Alomar, Jr. play here on tv when I was a kid". Jay said, "I remember watching Manny Ramirez hit bombs here before he went to Boston." We hung around a little bit more then decided it was time to eat. We grabbed a group photo right before we left. Tampa Bay beat Cleveland 6-3. We were at 19 stadiums with number 20 being just 16 short hours away.

As we headed over to Lounge 21, we saw Quicken Loans Arena. Jay said, "It's home to the Cleveland Cavaliers." I told the guys, "My favorite player, LeBron James used to play here, before he took his talents to South Beach." Pat said, "I wish we were going to South Beach again." I said, "Maybe in time, my friend, the Marlins do have a new ballpark coming soon." After dinner we went out a little bit in the Warehouse District downtown. The clubs and bars were very alive on this Saturday night. Lines formed outside of most of the clubs, while the locals enjoyed their weekend. It reminded me a lot of Old City in Philly, when we were 21. I reminded everyone we had an early bus to catch. I said, "Have fun, but not too much fun." I would have killed them if they didn't wake up in just a few hours.

Sunday morning came in a hurry, especially after a long travel day and some drinking. We didn't have much time to get to the Greyhound station. When the alarm went off I said, "Let's go fellas! This is why we're here." Eventually everyone was up and ready to go. We packed our bag and double-checked the hotel room. Once at the station, the guys grabbed some coffee and I had a bagel. I remember looking down at my ticket, and having the same reaction I did in Chicago. The ticket said Cleveland to Detroit. I looked at the guys and said, "We are literally everywhere." Jay said, "I never want this to end." We all agreed. We boarded the bus on time and had one stop in Toledo, Ohio before arriving in Detroit. The bus had a foul and unpleasant odor to it. At times it was unbearable. Pat joked, "Next time I'm booking the trip." I said, "We got a hell of a deal on this trip, and we'll be at 20 stadiums by the end of this day." The smell eventually faded as we were closing in on Detroit. We pulled into the bus station in Detroit and hailed a cab. On the ride over, Jay said, "Thank god we're off that bus." We all laughed. Pat said, "The road isn't cut out for everyone."

Comerica Park is a beautiful stadium in a rough part of town. The Motor City had been hit hard the last few years, through these tough economic times. Buildings downtown were abandoned and boarded up. Broken glass covered the sidewalks adjacent to them. A police officer guided traffic as game-time approached. Sirens of fire trucks could be faintly heard in the background. Ford Field was right next door. It was home to the Detroit Lions, and had hosted many Super Bowls and Thanksgiving day games.

I took some pictures of the Tiger statues outside as we scanned our tickets. They let us in with our backpacks on, stuffed with clothes. This was one thing I was worried about when I planned that trip. We went down to the dugout and had an usher take a photo for us. We tried to get to the games earlier to get our group shots, so we didn't have to disturb anyone during the games. We were all impressed with Comerica Park; it was in tip-top shape. We grabbed some lunch from the Big Cat Court, located near the first base side. We were surprised by the merry-go-round they had for the kids, along with other attractions around the concourse. Steve said, "It's a very kid friendly place." We went to our seats in the outfield and relaxed a little bit. We didn't stay the whole game, because we had a flight to catch back to Baltimore. The Blue Jays beat the Tigers in that game 5-3. I asked the cab driver, on the way back to the airport, if he could take us to "8 mile", home of the rapper Eminem. He responded, "There's nothing to see, guys." We arrived at the airport and prepared to fly back to Baltimore. We all agreed it was our craziest trip to date but a lot of fun. I turned to the boys and said, "How's 20 feel, guys?" Everyone said, "Great!" I said, "I can't wait for Cali." Steve would always say that the Cleveland Detroit trip was "a wild pitch".

On July 29th the Phillies would acquire Roy Oswalt from the Houston Astros at the trade deadline. This move would bolster our rotation for a deep run into October. We were poised for a third trip to the fall classic.

For the second straight summer, our most anticipated trip of the year was San Diego. They were the dog days of summer and it was scorching hot in South Philly. Children played under the fire hydrants in the streets to cool off. Local pools were packed with kids enjoying their summer break. I couldn't wait to sit on Mission Beach in San Diego, and stroll along the Walk of Fame on Hollywood Boulevard. I called Pat that morning and said, "We're going, going, back, back to Cali." Quoting the late, great rapper, The Notorious BIG. Pat's soon to be father-in-law offered us a ride to the airport, which we gladly accepted. Our excitement heightened as we boarded the nonstop airliner. In just six hours we would be back to our favorite state in America.

Our flight touched down in San Diego at approximately 11 am Pacific Time. We were anxious to get off the plane and to the hotel. After we checked in to the Holiday Inn Express, it was off to Mission Beach. We rented a gold Mustang convertible for the weekend. We kept the top off at all times. Jay said, "I love this car." We had the whole Saturday to enjoy, because we weren't going to Petco Park until Sunday, or to Dodger Stadium until Monday night.

Mission Beach looked just how we left it the year before. The sand felt so soft under our bare feet as we approached the water. Pat said, "The Pacific Ocean for the second straight year." The water was chilly but felt great on our hot skin. The California sun was really beating down on us that afternoon; luckily we had our Phillies hats on, and polarized sunglasses. We applied SPF 30 all over to protect us from burns and hopefully still get a tan. The light breeze off the ocean felt great. The guys said, "This is the life!" In the background, people of all ages and cultures enjoyed the adjacent boardwalk. It was filled with games, beach bars, and water attractions to keep cool. Many people were skateboarding and rollerblading along the boardwalk in their bikinis and swim trunks. Jay said, "Cali baby!" I said, "You gotta love the West Coast." After a few hours hanging on the beach, it was then time for dinner. We ate in Little Italy just like last year. Many people sat outside at the restaurants, enjoying this great summer night. The weather was perfect, at 70 degrees, with a light wind off the bay. After dinner, it was off to the Gaslamp District. Many people were out on this beautiful night in San Diego. Girls were dressed to impress, while guys had fresh haircuts and their best jewelry on. Lines formed outside of every bar and club in the area. Music blasted from cars' stereos as they passed in the streets, while cigarette smoke filled the sidewalks. After a few drinks I yawned and said, "I'm beat, fellas! I'm exhausted and I'm heading to bed." Everyone nodded and agreed. They said, "Let's gets ready for tomorrow. We still have the whole weekend here."

The next morning I woke up around 9am to a bunch of missed calls. I said, "I guess people forgot we're three hours behind over here." Thankfully I had my ringer off. Pat suggested breakfast at a small place around the corner from the hotel. The game was at one, so we took our time eating. Jay drove us down to stadium around 12:30, so we could get parking. We were extra excited this time around to visit Petco Park, because the Phillies were in town. As we entered I said, "Guys, you know I need another group pic." They said, "We got one last year." I responded, "Yeah, but not in our Phillies gear." They rolled their eyes at me. The pizza smell in the air had me craving lunch already even though I was still full from breakfast. As we scanned the park, we noticed a section full of Phillies fans. Pat said, "I think that's the trip the Phillies run every year." I said, "I bet our trip was half the price." Everyone laughed and agreed. It was sort of like déjà vu, because around the 6th inning Pat said, "The beach?" We all responded, "Definitely, let's go!" Steve said, "We already have that West Coast mentality." Pat already had his swim trunks on.

Mission Beach was very similar to the previous day. The sun was out, not a cloud in the sky. The mountains can be seen very clearly in the background. The beach was packed with people relaxing, smoking cigarettes or cigars and drinking beer. We walked around the pier that was connected to the boardwalk a little bit. We played some basketball games and cooled off a little, out of the sun. It was around 5pm when Pat said, "We probably should head back soon and get ready for dinner." We all nodded our heads in agreement. We took it easy that night because it was a Sunday and most bars would be quiet. We also were getting up early for our day in Los Angeles.

We set our alarms for 10am. My GPS said it was an hour and forty minutes to Hollywood, so I figured we would be there by noon. Jay wanted to drive, which we didn't have a problem with. I saw it in his eyes that he was falling in love with that car. We jumped on Interstate 5 with the top down, and not a care in the world. We were in our mid-twenties, driving through California in a convertible. Life couldn't get any better than this. We talked about our trip up to that point, and what we were going to do in L.A. all day. I told the guys, "Let's do Hollywood first, then we'll check out the Staples Center. After that we'll head over to Dodger Stadium."

As we got closer, we could see the Hollywood sign in the distance. Pat said, "This might be the greatest moment of my life." We all laughed. Jay parked on Hollywood Boulevard, and we walked on to see the Walk of Fame. I remember saying, "I don't see all the hype." Pat said, "Maybe we'll see some celebrities today." I said, "You never know out here." We had lunch at the Hollywood Hard Rock Cafe. The waitress told us that it had just opened a few weeks prior. After lunch we fought off some panhandlers who were trying to get us to take the Hollywood tour. I said, "We have our own car; we can just drive to those places." I stopped in a few souvenir shops and grabbed some things. We jumped back in the convertible and hit the roads. We cruised around through the rich parts of town, which included Beverly Hills and Sunset Boulevard. We stopped at the Staples Center, home to the Los Angeles Lakers. I took a picture of the Magic Johnson statue outside the arena. Jay said, "Magic wishes he was as good as Jordan." I replied, "MJ was the best, but LeBron is coming for him." Jay said, "No chance!" We both shared a laugh. The guys grabbed a quick coffee at a nearby Starbucks as game time approached. Jay punched in Dodger Stadium on the navigator and off we went.

There was light traffic in the area as we pulled up. Dodger Stadium has been the place fans call home since 1962. We parked in the lot and changed into our Phillies gear. Jay said, "I've always wanted to see this stadium; it's also called Chavez Ravine." We walked around the outside a little bit and noticed many palm trees surrounding it. I said, "I love California." Once inside, it reminded me of The Vet before the 1996 season, with its multi-colored seats in each level. We took a group picture in the second level behind home plate. Pat said, "Let's see what they have to eat." To our surprise, they had a "South Philly Cheesesteak." My eyes lit up and my mouth watered. I felt like I was back home. The guys grabbed a few Dodger Dogs and a couple of beers before we found our seats. We noticed beach balls being bounced around the crowd. Pat exclaimed, "It must be a Hollywood thing!"

Our ace Roy Halladay was pitching, so we felt confident about the game. I said to the guys, "It's a Monday night and we are in Dodger Stadium. This is unbelievable!" Everyone agreed. We weren't going to stay the whole game, because we had a two-hour ride back to San Diego. Just like in Boston, Jay pointed out the scoreboard. He said "Oh shit, we're getting no-hit." I said, "You gotta be kidding me." "This is a no-hitter we don't wanna see," Steve said. Pat said, "Now we gotta stay and see if they can break this up." We all agreed. In the 8th Shane Victorino finally slapped a ball to centerfield and ended the no-hitter. We exhaled and found the exits. Some fans did heckle us on the way out saying, "Go back to Philly, losers." I said, "I think they were salty because we eliminated them back-to-back years in the playoffs." The Phillies lost that game 3-0, recording just that one hit. On the way back Steve said, "This might of been the best trip ever." I said, "I think you're right, and if not it's pretty damn close."

The next morning we woke up around 5am to a pitch-black sky. We were exhausted, running on four hours sleep. Once we got ourselves together, we returned the Mustang to the rental company at the airport. When Jay handed the keys over, I swear I saw a tear in his eye. I said, "It's like the first day of school, Jay, you just have to let go." We all laughed. We were very close to missing our flight, due to the fact we were sleep-walking. On the flight home, I said, "We still have one more this year to see." Pat said, "The ATL!"

On October 2nd, we prepared for our "season finale" in Atlanta. In Philadelphia, the weather was changing over to fall. Windows were being decorated for Halloween, as my favorite holiday of the year approached. School was back in session full force, and summer was just a memory. This was the latest into a season we had been on a trip. We packed up the taxi in our long sleeves and jeans with our Phillies hats on. Postseason baseball was starting the next week, which had us excited. The Phillies had already clinched their fourth consecutive National League title earlier in the week. They would end the season with the best record in baseball at 97-65. Our plane landed around noon in Atlanta, and the local weather was warmer than Philly, at 75 degrees. Once we checked into the Sheraton hotel downtown, we were eager to see Turner Field. The park opened in 1996 for the Olympic Summer games, but the Braves didn't start playing there until 1997. On the cab ride over, we talked about the great Braves teams of the 90's. Jay said, "Their pitching was so dominating with Maddux, Smoltz, and Glavine." I said, "Don't forget about Chipper Jones and Fred McGriff." The Braves would win 14 straight division titles with one World Series trophy. We tipped our driver and got out in front of the stadium. I took a picture of the big Turner Field sign outside. This game didn't mean much to us because we had already clinched, but the Braves were still fighting for a wild card spot.

It was a sunny day at the park, with me shielding my eyes to see the scoreboard. Steve said, "Today is the Bobby Cox tribute game."

Bobby Cox is one of the most successful coaches of our time, I thought. It was nice to see him get an honor like this. After the ceremony, it was game time. We hung out at our seats and munched on some hot dogs. The Braves fans all did the Tomahawk chop in support of their team. Pat had his usual game beer in hand before the first pitch was thrown.

After a few innings, we wandered the concourse and took in all that Turner Field had to offer. Unfortunately, we got into a few arguments with the Braves fans. I think they were a little sore about us clinching the division already. I had a few words with one guy after he walked away, mumbling, "Phillies fans suck." I said, "Did you say something, buddy?" He yelled, "I can't hear you." I ran in his face and yelled back, "Can you hear me now, asshole?" I could smell the beer and cigarettes on his breath. "Have fun making the playoffs," I said sarcastically. He said, "Whatever, dude." After a moment or two, a bunch of people stepped in between us and said, "Walk away, guys!" Steve said, "Let's enjoy the game and the stadium." We experienced a little trash talk at Citi Field in New York, but this was the first time that it almost escalated into a fight. The Phillies won the game 7-0. After things calmed down a bit, we decided to head back to the hotel. That night we relaxed at a local bar downtown and had a few cold drinks. We took it easy, considering we had another whole day there.

The next morning, Pat suggested that we have breakfast at Gladys Knight's Waffle House on Peachtree Street. We waited in line for an hour, at which point I told Pat, "McDonald's was just down the street." I was frigging starving at that point. There was a sign on the door that said "no guns allowed". We turned to Pat and asked, "Is this a safe place?" He chuckled and said, "It will be fine." We finally got seated, after a truly long wait. I remember I had the "Midnight Express", which consisted of fried chicken and waffles. The guys had fresh coffee along with their meal. After breakfast, we headed down to the Georgia Aquarium and Atlanta's "World of Coca-Cola". Many tourists roamed the area, taking pictures of the exteriors. We eventually passed by the Georgia Dome, which is home to the Atlanta Falcons. The guys said, "Another great trip! 22 down! I can't wait for next year!"

The Phillies would host the Cincinnati Reds in the NLDS. Roy Halladay would throw a no-hitter in his first career playoff start. He was the first pitcher since Don Larsen to throw a no-hitter in the playoffs. Cole Hamels would dominate in game three, as the Phillies swept out the Reds in the first round.

The Phillies would be in the NLCS for the third straight season. They would host the red-hot San Francisco Giants. The Giants would beat the Phillies in six games and go on to win the World Series. Ryan Howard would get caught looking on a called strike three to end the series, and the season. As fans, we were disappointed, but we knew how hard it was to reach the World Series three years in a row. We ourselves had reached 22 stadiums by the end of this season. Our goal of 30 was getting closer and closer.

Jay, Pat, Me & Steve at Chase Field in Phoenix, AZ

The pool in Chase Field

Me, Pat, Jay & Steve at Coors Field in Denver, CO

The fountains in centerfield at Coors Field

16th Street Mall in downtown Denver

Rooftop view from Hotel VQ

Progressive Field in Cleveland, OH

The Rock & Roll Hall of Fame in Cleveland, OH

Comerica Park in Detroit, MI

Comerica Park in Detroit, MI

Petco Park in San Diego, CA

Little Italy in San Diego

Mission Beach in San Diego, CA

Mission Beach Boardwalk

Dodger Stadium in Los Angeles, CA

Me & Pat in the gold Mustang convertible

The Hollywood Sign

Staples Center home to the LA Lakers

Home of the Braves

Me, Steve, Pat and Jay at Turner Field in Atlanta, GA

The World of Coca Cola

The Georgia Aquarium

Out for the Season

The 2010 season provided us with many laughs and adventures. We were now at an even 22 stadiums visited. In November 2010, I started to check out what our remaining options were. It was getting harder now, since there were just eight left. I was hoping to do five trips, and get us to 27. Kansas City was most likely for April. I figured we would visit Seattle in June, because the Phillies would be in town. I also noticed that the Phillies were playing Toronto on the weekend of July 4th. I thought, that could be a trip we can drive to, so we can save some money. So I had three possible stadium trips planned, with intentions of doing two more later in the year. Of course I had to run this by the group, because it could get pricey.

I gave Steve a call, and ran him through our options, and he said, "Looks good to me! I'm glad that the Phillies are playing." I said, "Yeah, me too!" The Phillies were coming off of four straight division titles at the time, so I wanted to see them as much as possible. I texted Pat, "Call me, it's about our 2011 schedule." He called me back a little later in the day and said, "I don't have a problem with it so far." I was like, "Great!" Over the years, Pat would make me hang for an answer sometimes, so his instant response of yes made me smile. I always wondered if the plans I put in place were too intense or too expensive. Sometimes it was hard to get everyone on the same page, because of work schedules, girlfriends, and finances. Last but not least was Jay. I figured I didn't even have to call him; he was always in no matter what the date or the price.

The phone rang. "Hello," I said. Jay said, "What's up, man?" I replied, "Nothing much. I was going over the 2011 baseball schedule and wanted to get your feedback on it." Jay responded, "You're gonna kill me." I quickly asked, "What's wrong?" He said, "I'm sorry! I just started this new job, and getting time off is gonna be hard. I won't be able to do any trips this year." I replied, "Shit!" His response was, "Don't let me hold you guys back. Go, and have fun, and I'll eventually make them up." I said, "No problem Jay, I'll talk to ya soon." So one of our men was out for the season. I informed Steve and Pat. They were disappointed, but understood that work comes first. We prepared for the season, but really felt bad because we were a man down.

Cliff Lee, a fan favorite who was traded in the previous season, resigned for a five-year deal worth $125 million. I remember my brother Mark woke me up at midnight to tell me the news. I was shaking in excitement, as I turned on ESPN. We now had the most feared rotation in all of baseball, with Roy Halladay, Cliff Lee, Cole Hamels and Roy Oswalt. They were called the "Four Aces." We were clear-cut favorites to win the World Series. Our all star outfielder Jayson Werth signed as a free agent with the Washington Nationals for a seven-year deal worth $126 million. Phillies fans were outraged that he signed a contract with a division rival. I couldn't blame him for taking the money. After a really long and cold winter in Philly, it was finally spring time. Baseball was back!!!

On April 30th, 2011 it was time for us to go to Kansas City, Missouri. Pat, Steve, and I took a cab to the airport early that morning. It will still a weird feeling, not having Jay there. It was the same feeling I had in St. Louis with Pat missing. We had a strong bond together, and our friendship grew stronger after each trip. I loved the camaraderie. We all mournfully said, "We'll have a drink for him." During the trip, Steve would do impersonations of Jay, so in a way it felt like he was still there. Upon arrival, we checked into our hotel, then headed to the Country Club Plaza. Kansas City had a very large outdoor mall, with many shops and restaurants to offer. Many people held shopping bags in their hands, while others walked their dogs along the crowded sidewalks. We had some ice cream from Cold Stone and talked about the upcoming game. Pat said, "The Royals have a young and upcoming team." We agreed. Little did we know they would be World Series champions in just a few short years. "They remind me of the 2008 Phillies," Steve said. I responded, "Definitely." It was around 5pm, and we decided it was time to head over to Kauffman Stadium.

Kauffman Stadium was an older park, not as old as Fenway Park or Wrigley Field, though it had a retro feel to it. It was often referred to as "The K", named after founding owner Ewing Kauffman and built in 1973. The Royals were playing their division rivals, the Minnesota Twins. As we arrived, we also noticed Arrowhead Stadium, home to the Kansas City Chiefs, just across the parking lot. Fans, dressed in their royal blue jerseys and hats, poured into the stadiums entrance. The large scoreboard in centerfield caught my eye first. It had a gigantic gold crown on top of it. We approached the first concession we saw and stood in line. The lady asked me, "Can I help you sir?" I said, "Yes, can I have two hot dogs and a large Coca-Cola, please?" She replied, "Coming right up!" Pat said, "I'll take the same, and a Budweiser." The lady responded, "Thanks guys! Enjoy the game!" Pat loved his beer. There were times he told us we weren't men if we didn't drink at every game. I often said, "I hate those people who come to the game just to drink; I come for the game." Steve agreed. Steve said, "Or those people who just post it on Facebook, but could care less about the game." I couldn't have agreed more. These were the types of things we often said over the course of time. We always enjoyed our time together, and had as much fun as possible. We liked to break each other's chops once in a while.

After we ate, I suggested we go see the fountains in the outfield. They shot up every time a Royals player would hit a home run. Around the third inning, we saw them in action and got sprayed with the light mist on that spring night in Missouri. We walked around a bit and tried to see everything the stadium had to offer. I always wore my Phillies hat, so occasionally other fans would ask me if I was from Philadelphia. I would tell them that we were doing all 30 stadiums, which they thought was great. I would always get asked which was my favorite one, and I would always reply, "All of them!" The Royals won the game 11-2.

After the game we went out for some drinks in the Kansas City Power & Light District. People of all ages packed the club area, enjoying the great spring night. We were watching the Phillies game in prime time at a local sports bar when the news broke that Osama Bin Laden had been killed. Chants of "USA, USA, USA!" carried out from Citizens Bank Park back in Philly. We were proud to be Americans. It was a big moment in our country's history.

Monday approached us fast, on that beautiful Kansas City morning. We walked around the corner from our hotel, as rush hour traffic passed us by. Horns honked and police sirens could be heard in the distance. People in suits and dresses filled the streets as they were preparing for the new work week ahead of them. We had breakfast at a place named Winstead's. I remember the name so vividly because I said to the guys, "Winsteads?, Let's eat somewhere instead." The smell of coffee and French toast filled the air in this large diner. The food was actually great, though. We flew home later that day. It still felt weird not having Jay on that flight with us. I kept feeling like we were missing something the whole trip. I remember Jay calling me that Monday night, asking me how the trip was. I told him, "Fun, but not the same without ya'."

It was June 18th and our next trip was to Seattle, Washington. We intended to fly out of BWI airport again, like we did the previous year. This trip included us taking the "Megabus" to Baltimore, flying from BWI to Houston, and then continuing from Houston to Seattle. On the return trip, it was Seattle to Houston, Houston to Newark, followed by a Megabus back to Philly from Newark. I thought to myself that I couldn't believe Steve and Pat agreed to it.

After a really long and drawn out travel day, we finally arrived in Seattle around 10pm local time. Our body clocks were at 1am and we were exhausted. I was ready for bed a long time ago. While driving in the cab we saw Safeco Field, home of the Mariners, and also CenturyLink Field, home to the Seahawks, through the window. There was a little drizzle falling on the windshield of the taxi. Seattle is known for its share of rain. I said to the guys, "I'm tired! I hope I'm not going to be Sleepless in Seattle," referring to the Tom Hanks and Meg Ryan movie. They laughed. We took quick showers and immediately laid on our perfectly-made beds for the night.

The next morning, we saw the famous Space Needle hovering above the city. Pat said, "We'll check that out tomorrow." It was almost game time, as the clouds moved in. I said, "No need to worry about the weather! Safeco has a dome." We went back to the hotel and changed into our Phillies attire. I had my Cliff Lee jersey on. I was so happy he was back with us. We arrived at Safeco Field around 12:30pm to see players stretching and warming up on the field. The field crew was prepping, hosing down the infield. We could smell the pine tar as it was being applied to the bats. Steve said, "There's Cliff Lee!" I went down to the field level and yelled, "Cliff, Cliff, Cliff." I'm surprised security didn't escort me out. I felt like a little kid at Veterans Stadium all over again. I waived my Phillies jersey in the air to grab his attention. Phillies starting pitcher Kyle Kendrick was speaking with his family while I was still on the field level. They wished him good luck as he prepared for the game.

We had fairly good seats on the third base side closer to home plate. We also had a great view of the Seattle skyline. I turned to the boys and said, "24 stadiums, how's it feel?" They said, "Great!" Steve said, "I wish Jay could have been here, though." Pat and I both agreed. The aroma of hot dogs and popcorn filled the air, which had my stomach rumbling. I asked the guys if they wanted anything from the concourse and they replied, "Nah, we're good, thanks." I devoured two hot dogs like I'd never eaten before. Safeco Field was huge, with many power alleys. Pat said, "I'm sure a lot of triples are hit here." Steve said, "This is definitely a pitchers park." The Phillies were trailing the whole game, in this fast-paced Interleague play match-up. They would eventually lose the game 2-0. We exited the stadium and headed back to our hotel. We Face-Timed Jay on my iPhone and said, "We miss you here." He replied, "I'm sorry, but have fun!"

The next morning the sky was pitch-gray, with a chance of rain, and it was a cool 65 degrees. It was off to the Space Needle, which was barely visible in the sky. The Space Needle is a observation deck which was built in the Seattle Center for the 1962 World's Fair. It is iconic in Seattle, Washington. "I've seen this is so many times in movies," I said. We took a small elevator up to the top, which was 600 feet in the air. Pat said, "Luckily we aren't afraid of heights." I remember feeling a bit nauseated, as the structure swayed in the wind. It reminded me a lot of the Gateway Arch in St. Louis. We had astonishing views of the downtown Seattle skyline, as well as of the

Olympic and Cascade Mountains, Mount Rainier and Mount Baker. Pat said, "I think we can see Vancouver from here." They had a small gift shop on the top floor, where we purchased some collectibles and keepsakes. Steve said, "Let's go see the original Starbucks." We took the small elevator back down to the ground floor, and hailed a cab to the Elliott Bay waterfront.

Starbucks originated in Seattle at the Pike Place Market, which overlooks the Elliott Bay waterfront. It opened in 1971 and has been a smash hit ever since. Starbucks is pretty much on every corner in every city in the United States. I'm not a big coffee drinker, but I knew Pat and Steve wanted to see it. The smell of fresh coffee filled the store, as we waited 15 minutes in line. They savored the taste of their drinks as we walked along the water front. Pat said, "Mmm so good." Steve said, "I love fresh coffee." It was still hazy and overcast with a chance of rain at any time, but that didn't stop us from enjoying ourselves. Before we knew it, the weekend was over and it was time to head back east. The guys said, "We really enjoyed the Pacific Northwest." I agreed. Our flight home stopped in Houston then Newark. We then took the Megabus back to Philly, arriving home at 1am. We were extremely tired, but excited to have knocked out our 24th ballpark. The Phillies were playing the Blue Jays in Toronto in just a few weeks, on July 4th weekend.

It was July 4th and one of the biggest holidays of the year. It was our nation's Independence Day. Many families flocked down the shore, hoping to catch a great weekend at the beach. We decided to leave the country for this holiday weekend, to watch our beloved Phillies play a weekend series in Canada.

A friend of ours dropped us off outside the Hertz rental car at the Philly airport. I signed the necessary documents and we jumped on the road around 9am and headed for Toronto. I made sure that everyone had their passports in hand so we could cross the border with no problems. Last thing I wanted was for somebody not to be allowed in for any reason. I joked and said, "Nobody has any warrants out for their arrest right?" Pat and Steve laughed. My GPS said eight hours. That was without stops for gas or food. We were cruising along, just talking about our adventures up to that point. We were excited to see our 25th individual stadium, and our first in a different country. The Phillies were playing at 1pm, so we turned the radio on and tuned in to the matinee. Later on that day, around 6pm, we approached the border crossing. It was at least a one-hour wait to cross over into Canada. The flags of many countries flew above us. Steve said, "Come on, I gotta pee." Eventually it was our turn. The Border Patrol guard asked us about our visit as he checked our passports. We told him we were in from Philadelphia to see the Blue Jays take on the Phillies. He inspected our trunk and told us we were good to go. As we sped off, he said, "Let's go Jays." We laughed and proceeded down the road.

After we crossed the border I noticed the speed limit signs were in kilometers. I forgot that every country in the world uses the metric system, besides the United States. My cell phone service then switched from AT&T to the Rodgers Network. I received a text saying, "Roaming charges will now apply." Out of nowhere, our brand new rental car started acted funny. The turn signals were flickering off and on, while the radio changed channels without direction. I was puzzled at what was going on. The guys said, "You gotta be kidding me, this is why we rented a car, to avoid a vehicle mishap." The engine started to putt like it was out of gas, and it sounded like we were going to stall. It started shaking and I started to lose horsepower. I was just hoping to make it to the hotel and then we could worry about it later. I started having flashbacks to D.C. back in 2008, when my car almost broke down. We all remained calm then the lady on the GPS said, "Five minutes until you have reached your destination." I said, "I hope we have five minutes! I really don't want to break down." We putted into the hotel a few minutes later, and I told the valet driver, "Good luck, it's a piece of shit." We proceeded to check in and I later called the rental company for a new car. They told me to swap out the car first thing in the morning, which we did.

The next morning, after swapping out rental cars, we proceeded to the Rogers Centre, the home of the Toronto Blue Jays. We were very surprised to see how much Toronto resembled an American city. We did convert our money over to Canadian dollars. For every $60 American dollars we received $54 Canadian dollars. Steve said, "So much for the value of the dollar." As we walked closer to the stadium, we could see the CN Tower filling up the Toronto skyline. Pat said, "It looks like a skyscraper in New York." The CN Tower opened in 1974 and is the third-largest building in the world at 1815 feet. It has an observation deck and a communications tower. I snapped some great pictures as we approached the former Skydome. The Rogers Centre has been home to the Blue Jays since 1989. I remember watching the 1993 Blue Jays beat the Phillies in Game 6 of the World Series here, on television. It was extra hot and humid on this July 4th weekend. We were constantly taking our

Phillies hats off and wiping the sweat from our heads. I couldn't wait to shower after the game. We did our usual tour around the ballpark, and eventually found our seats along the first base side. The smell of burgers, steaks and fries filled the concourse, making our stomachs growl. I was excited to see my favorite Phillies pitcher Cliff Lee start this game. Steve said, "That's crazy, that there is a hotel in center field." I responded, "I tried to book it but it was completely full." Pat grabbed us some cold beers for that sticky summer day.

It was a little weird that we were in another country for our nation's Independence Day, but baseball was more important to us than the beach that weekend. The stadium announcer said "Ladies and gentlemen, please rise for the national anthems of both countries." We removed our hats, while a young lady sang "Oh, Canada!" and "The Star-Spangled Banner". Cheers erupted from the sold-out crowd. The place was packed with both Phillies and Blue Jays fans. The CN Tower was visible from home plate. It was a back-and-forth contest between the two clubs, but the Blue Jays hit a few home runs to seal the deal. "Cliff Lee didn't pitch well in this game," I said. The guys replied, "We'll get them next time." I turned to Steve and Pat and said, "25 down, boys, 5 to go." It was an amazing feeling, being this close to the end. As we exited the stadium, Pat and Steve suggested coffee. We found a Starbucks not too far from our hotel. Due to the roaming charges on our phones, we kept them on airplane mode most of the trip. It felt good being disconnected from the world for a short time. As the free Wi-Fi connected, our phones exploded with emails, texts and voicemails from family and friends. Pat said, "Let's grab some dinner and head over to Dundas Square."

We enjoyed our final night in Toronto at Yonge-Dundas Square. It was very similar to Times Square in New York City. Advertisements and flashing billboards filled the sides of buildings. People crossed the streets, as car horns honked at them. Kids skateboarded off the ramps nearby. We found a local pub that served pint-sized beers. We had some dinner and decided to head back to the hotel. We had a long drive home the next day.

We hit the road early, anticipating a nine-hour ride back. I said to the guys, "It's a shame we didn't have time to see Niagara Falls." As the next exit sign approached, we saw that it said, "Niagara Falls next right". I smiled from ear to ear and said, "You wanna go? We're in no rush to get home." They agreed, and we turned right. Many hotels and casinos surrounded the falls, providing guests with amazing views.

Niagara Falls was formed when glaciers receded at the end of the last ice age. The water from the newly formed Great Lakes made a path into the Niagara Escarpment en route to the Atlantic Ocean. We parked in a lot for $20 dollars and proceeded to the observation decks. We could hear and see the water rumbling as it fell from the heights. I took some great pictures and videos of the falls, there on the Canadian side. The cool mist felt great on our sweaty skin on that hot, humid day. Some people were even brave enough to ride on the Maid of the Mist, a boat that comes very close to the base of the falls. I said, "Not me! I'm scared of the water; with my luck it will tip over." After about an hour or so I said, "We probably should get back on the road." Everyone nodded and said, "Yeah lets head back to the United States. The line through the border crossing wasn't as bad as it was coming into Canada. The Border Patrol agent checked our passports and asked us a few questions. They inspected our trunk for any tobacco, such as Cuban Cigars, which are illegal here in the States. Everything checked out okay and we were en route to Philadelphia. We chatted on the way home about what we could do next. I didn't have anything lined up yet, but that could change in a heartbeat. We only had five options left, so it was getting tricky to find great deals. I knew I had to get creative and maybe find us a trip on which we could see two at once. As we pulled into Philadelphia and returned our rental car, it hit me. I knew what our next move would be. The question was how much it would cost us. Pat, Steve, and I enjoyed a nice juicy Pat's Steak on this tail end of the July 4th weekend back in Philly.

On July 29th, the Philadelphia Phillies acquired right fielder Hunter Pence, from the Houston Astros. Former Phillies GM Ed Wade struck a deal with current Phillies GM Ruben Amaro, Jr. It was a mega deal that send four talented prospects to the Astros. Pence instantly became a fan favorite with his corky batting stance, and unorthodox baseball antics. The Phillies were 50-30 at the time, and had their minds set on October baseball.

We were in the dog days of summer in Philadelphia. Heat waves were clobbering the East Coast left and right. The news told us to check on our elders, while kids roamed the streets, free of school for at least six more weeks. Some people had packed up and vacationed down the shore for the summer, hoping to get that perfect tan. Meanwhile, the Phillies were the best team in baseball by far. Myself, I was back at home working on our next trip. I was searching the internet night and day looking for the right deal. I was eyeing San Francisco. Most airlines drop their prices on Monday and Tuesday nights. I was repeatedly checking the websites for that perfect trip to fall into my lap.

Finally one night I checked again and the airfare was halved. I combined it with a hotel and saw a grand total. I frantically called Steve up with the news. He said, "It sounds good, but it's still a little expensive." I told him, "Yeah that true, but we only have five stadiums left. Our options are slim." He said, "Ok, check with Pat and see what he says." I called Pat, and he agreed it was a tad pricey for just one trip. So I had to sweeten the deal somehow. I realized that Oakland was just 45 minutes from downtown San Francisco. That was the key. I had to find a weekend where both the Giants and Athletics were playing at home. There was literally just one weekend on which that was true, and it was Labor Day weekend. I figured that if I could get two stadiums done on the same trip, then the price of $600 dollars for airfare and hotel wouldn't seem so bad. I told Pat and Steve the new plan and they agreed. The price was worth it, if we could reach 27 stadiums visited by the end of 2011. I punched in my credit card number and finalized the trip just a few hours later.

About a week later I got a call from Steve. I answered, "What up, Steve?" He had so much energy in his voice. He responded, "You're not gonna believe this! Jay said he wants to come on the trip. I just spoke with him." I said, "Seriously? That's great!" Steve said, "Can you find him the same price?" I said, "I'm sure I can find him the same deal." We hung up and I rushed to the computer. I was able to find him the exact same price as ours, and the same flights. I was thrilled we were going to have the original four guys back together in California. It felt like old times again. I couldn't wait until Labor Day.

Labor Day arrived in a hurry, marking the end of the summer. Parents bought their children new supplies and uniforms for the upcoming school year. The weather was slowly changing, after the brutal summer we had had. The taxi picked us up bright and early. I said, "The crew is back!" I've wanted to visit San Francisco my whole life. I remember watching the 49ers play at Candlestick Park, on Sunday afternoons on television as a kid. I grew up watching the hit sitcom "Full House", which is based in the Bay Area. I told the guys I had found the actual house they used for the exterior shots of the show. The guys said, "Nice, we'll definitely visit it." I also told them Alcatraz was a must. I've been interested in the famous prison, also known as "The Rock", my whole life. We boarded our flight and entertained ourselves for the six hours. Steve said, "I can't wait to make it 27 stadiums." We all agreed.

We arrived around noon local time. We took a cab to our amazing hotel downtown. Steve said, "This might be the best hotel you've ever booked." We didn't have any games planned for the first day. I suggested visiting the house from "Full House". The guys said, "Sounds good!" Our taxi pulled up at 1709 Broderick Street. "That's it!" I yelled. I got out and had the cab driver take a group picture of us outside the Tanners' residence. Later on we arrived at Alamo Park, which stood across the street from the "Painted Ladies", a famous row of Victorian houses. I said, "These were used in the intro of the TV show." These houses were beautiful, and very expensive-looking.

Many tourists filled the park, trying to capture that perfect picture on their Smartphones. People jogged past us with their headphones on, enjoying the nice weather. Dogs ran around like it was their very own backyard. The light breeze felt great, with the California sun out. Pat said, "We should check out Fisherman's Wharf. We can see Alcatraz from there." We jumped in another taxi and headed there. We approached a huge sign that said Fisherman's Wharf. Many tourists from all over the world were there on this holiday weekend. We walked a few steps and noticed a sign for Alcatraz Tours. I asked the lady at that window politely, "Four tickets please." She responded, "I'm sorry, but we're all sold out today." I said, "Damn!" She replied, "Sir, we still offer the boat tour, which goes around Alcatraz Island, and under the Golden Gate Bridge." I turned to the guys and they said, "That's fine. We'll take them."

The wind was strong off the water as our ferry took off. Our hoodies and sweatshirts were flapping around. Pat's hat almost flew into the water. It was first going to take us underneath the famous bridge, then encircle Alcatraz. On the bumpy ride out, we talked about the movie "Escape from Alcatraz". Steve said, "Do you think it's possible to escape?" I said, "I guess anything is possible, but they never found those guys who escaped years ago." The prison once hosted the notorious gangster Al Capone. Over the years, the prison cost too much money to keep up and maintain, so it closed for good in 1963, the same year JFK was assassinated. The tour guide got on his megaphone and said, "Folks, above you is the breathtaking Golden Gate Bridge." I quickly took my iPhone out and snapped pictures. Pat said, "Tomorrow we'll walk the bridge."

The ferry made a wide turn after it passed the bridge, heading back in the direction of Alcatraz Island. It crept up in the distance as our ferry picked up speed. I said, "Going to prison is hard enough, let alone being trapped on an island at the same time." The guys said, "Yeah that must have been hard time to do." Our ferry docked, and it was almost game time.

On television, AT&T Park is beautiful. In person it's even better. We entered through the Willie Mays gate, and there wasn't a cloud in the sky. The Giants were hosting the Diamondbacks that night. We walked around the tiny concourse to the outfield. There were many people in their kayaks sitting around in McCovey Cove, named after Giants great Willie McCovey. Many Barry Bonds home run balls ended up there, especially during his record-setting years. As the breeze off the water hit us in the face I said, "This is amazing! This could be the nicest stadium we've been to." The guys said, "You're right, this is pretty." We took a picture on a replica trolley in the outfield, then searched for some good food to eat. Pat said, "I'm hungry. I've heard they have great crab here." I said, "I'll probably grab a hot dog." Pat found Crazy Crab'z in the center field concourse. He spent $17 dollars on the crab, but said they were delicious and worth every penny. Jay and Steve picked up some food at the next concession stand, closer to our seats. From our seats we could see the monstrous Coca-Cola bottle in the outfield, along with the gigantic baseball glove. I said to the guys, "This park is unbelievable." In right field they had a sign that said, "Splash Hits". "Every time someone hits McCovey Cove with a home run ball that number changes," Steve said. We grabbed a few drinks and enjoyed the rest of the game. Arizona won the game 7-2.

The next morning it was a chilly 47 degrees. After breakfast, we took the train over to Oakland to see the Athletics play at the Coliseum. The train was packed with A's fans. Steve said sarcastically, "I think we're going the right way." We laughed. The voice on the speakers said, "Next stop, Oakland Coliseum." We arrived at the stadium around 12:30 pm. We walked through the large tunnel leading into it. Many ticket scalpers asked us if we needed tickets. I responded, "Thanks, we already have them." I always purchased game tickets in advance. I never wanted to take a chance that a game would be sold out. Jay said, "This is one of the few stadiums left that host both football and baseball." The circular structure reminded me of Veterans Stadium a lot; The Vet also hosted baseball and football. There was a good crowd in attendance, despite their record in the standings. The upper deck was closed during baseball games, just like many stadiums do when the teams are struggling to draw fans. The A's were hosting the Seattle Mariners. I turned to the boys and said, "27!" I couldn't believe we were only three away from our goal.

We could smell hot sausage sandwiches as we walked around. We all agreed to eat some before we headed to our seats. I took a bunch of pictures of the stadium before we left. We only stayed five innings, because we were eager to walk The Golden Gate Bridge on our final day in San Francisco. As we left, we could see Oracle Arena right next door, home of the Golden State Warriors. Jay said, "Stephen Curry is supposed to be the next big star in the NBA." I replied, "Yeah I've heard the same thing. The Warriors are gonna be good in a few years." We asked a security guard how to get back on the train, and he pointed us in the right direction. He also said,

"Here's my .45; don't forget we're in Oakland." We looked at him blankly, and then he busted out laughing. He said, "Don't worry, you'll be fine." We were back in San Fran within 35 minutes.

The Golden Gate Bridge is a suspension bridge that opened in 1937. It has been featured in many movies and television shows over the years. The walkway on the bridge was packed with people, riding their bikes or walking across. The views were incredible. Mountains were visible in the distance, and to our right we could see Alcatraz Island. Pat said, "It looks smaller from up here." The wind gained strength, but we held on to our clothing and hats. Many cars zipped by us as we were walking across. I remember turning to the guys and saying, "Never in my life did I think I would be walking the Golden Gate Bridge with 3 of my close friends, because of baseball." We walked two-thirds of the way, then turned back to the city. People on bikes and rollerblades zoomed passed, nearly crashing into us a few times. Many people also jogged across the bridge on that beautiful, windy day in the Bay Area.

The next morning we boarded our flight, which signaled the end of another amazing season. We had now visited 27 stadiums, with only three left to go. We couldn't wait to get home and see the Phillies play playoff baseball. We were hoping for another World Series title.

The Phillies clinched their 5th straight National League title, with the best record in all of baseball at 102-60. Despite the best record and home field advantage, the Phillies would lose in the first round to the St. Louis Cardinals, in 5 games. Ryan Howard would rupture his Achilles tendon on the final play of the season. The St.Louis Cardinals would go on to win the World Series against the Texas Rangers.

Me, Steve & Pat at Kauffman Stadium in Kansas City, MO

The fountains at Kauffman Stadium in the Outfield

Safeco Field in Seattle, WA

The Space Needle in Seattle, WA

View from the top of the Space Needle

The original Starbucks

Rogers Centre – Home of the Blue Jays

The Rogers Centre in Toronto, ON

Stephen Pagano

The CN Tower visible from the Rogers Centre

Yonge-Dundas Square

Niagara Falls from the Canadian Side

The Mist of the Falls

AT&T Park in San Francisco, CA

The Trolley in centerfield at AT&T Park

The Oakland Coliseum

Jay, Steve, Pat & Me at the Oakland Coliseum

The Golden Gate Bridge

Alcatraz Island

The Painted Ladies in Alamo Park

Full House

The Home Stretch

I n 2012, we had only three ballparks left. There was the Rangers Ballpark in Arlington, Texas, formerly known as "The Ballpark" and now known as Globe Life Park, home of the Texas Rangers. There was Great American Ballpark in Cincinnati, home of the Reds. Finally, there was Target Field in Minneapolis, home to the Minnesota Twins. The only question was, would we do them all in one season or would we save one for 2013? We were closing in on our goal. After consulting with the guys, we chose to see two in 2012 and one in 2013. We decided to fly to Dallas, Tx to see the Rangers in April and drive to Cincinnati in September to see the Reds play.

On April 28th, 2012 our flight landed in Dallas, Texas. Steve said, "I'm happy to be back in Texas; I really enjoyed Houston in 2009." I was extra excited to be in Dallas to see the Sixth Floor Museum. It was located on Elm Street, the former Texas School Book Depository. It was infamous, because President John F. Kennedy was assassinated in Dealey Plaza from a sixth floor window on November 22, 1963.

The Texas sun was extra brutal on us that afternoon. I was having flashbacks to Houston in 2009. As we approached Elm Street in Dealey Plaza, I started to get goosebumps. I said to Steve, "I've seen this street a thousand times in books and documentaries." It was a weird feeling, because I knew a president of the United States was killed on this very block. We entered the museum and purchased our tickets with an audio set included. We all toured the sixth floor and took our time examining every exhibit. I stared out of the same window from which Lee Harvey Oswald allegedly shot and killed President JFK. I could see the trees swaying in the wind before the old Texas School Book Depository. Steve and I talked about different conspiracy theories surrounding the President's death. I was very fascinated with all of these theories and explanations about that tragic day on November 23, 1963. We exited the museum through a gift shop, where we bought replica newspapers from that fatal day in Dallas. Pat said, "Let's head back to the hotel and prepare for the game in Arlington."

Later that night, the Rangers were playing in prime time on ESPN. Jay said, "This reminds me of that Yankees game we saw back in '06 in prime time." Our taxi ride to Arlington was around thirty minutes or so. We joked with the driver and asked him about good bars in the city. He gave us some suggestions and recommendations. He talked about some crazy passengers he had picked up on late nights. We all shared a laugh as he dropped us off.

"The Ballpark" in Arlington opened in 1994. The Rangers were hosting the Tampa Bay Rays. Right across their parking lot was brand new Cowboy Stadium, owned by billionaire Jerry Jones. I snapped a few pictures of the gigantic football stadium before we entered. I joked with Jay about the Cowboys, since he was a diehard Eagles fan. Once inside we could hear our stomachs growling. I said, "I heard they have two-foot hot dogs here. I have seen them on television." Pat said, "No chance, they might kill us." We all laughed. Pat was the guy in the group who ate healthy and worked out a lot. We decided to skip eating the massive hot dog, as Pat preferred.

Ranger's fans packed the concourse as we were finding our seats for the game. We found our seats, beers in our hands. We were happy to be in another city to see another stadium. Steve said, "28! Two more to go." The Rangers fans were filled with a lot of energy and excitement. They were back-to-back American League Champions, something we could relate to. We took our traditional picture before heading to the team store. Like clockwork I bought my postcard and Pat bought his shot glass. The Rays beat the Rangers 5-2 in this American League showdown. After the game, Pat found us a nice sports bar to hang out at to watch the Dallas Mavericks playoff game. We enjoyed a couple of ice-cold brews and relaxed in the heart of Dallas. Steve said, "I love the Texas mentality."

The Phillies had a horrific start in 2012, which made them sellers at the trade deadline. They traded away fan favorite center fielder Shane Victorino as the team was going in another direction. They also traded right fielder Hunter Pence, whom they acquired the previous season, to the San Francisco Giants. This had been the first time in five years that we weren't experiencing winning baseball.

On June 16th, Pat would be the first guy out of the group who got married. He wed his longtime girlfriend of 10 years, Jackie. It was a great wedding, and so was the reception that followed. We were happy for our good friend, as we were getting older and growing up.

In September we planned to visit our 29th ballpark, in Cincinnati. We opted to drive to Ohio, since it was cheaper than flying. We rented a car from the airport and I hoped for better luck than we had the last time we rented one. We braced ourselves for a nine-hour drive. Along the way, the long road trip reminded us of our visits to Pittsburgh and Toronto. We arrived in Cincinnati around 7 pm on a Saturday night. The weather was crappy, with dark clouds hanging over the city. My first thought was to hope they would not postpone the game the next day. We were too close to our goal for a rainout. We decided to have dinner in Fountain Square.

Fountain Square was built in 1871. It featured many restaurants, shops, hotels, and bars. Many locals were skateboarding on that damp and rainy night. We walked around, dodging puddles in the street, with umbrellas up. After having a great dinner in Fountain Square, we found a nice bar not too far away. The rain eased up as we walked back to our hotel. We shot some pool and played some darts in the lobby sports bar. I said, "Eightball corner pocket!" as I won the game. The music blasted from the speakers as our night was winding down. We called it a night early, since we had driven almost 10 hours that day. We were really hoping the Reds would play the game the next day at 1 pm.

The next morning it was very overcast, with a light drizzle falling on the Cincinnati area. I opened our drapes in the hotel room and said, "Shit, I hope they get this game in." This was the last game of the series, and the Reds were going on the road afterward. We had only one shot to see Great American Ballpark, and that was that day's game. After a late breakfast, we took a short cab ride over to the stadium. I took a picture of the large sign outside that said Great American Ball Park. Many fans were piling in, with their Reds and Phillies attire on. We scanned our tickets and entered the home of the Reds. The infield was covered with the tarp, to prevent puddles from forming on the playing dirt. The sky was dark gray with light rain falling as the first pitch was thrown. We could barely see the smokestacks in center field. I said to Steve, "I wonder if they will hand out ponchos like they did in Baltimore?" He said, "They would be perfect for this game."

There was a light breeze coming off the Ohio River during the game. Barely in view was the suspension bridge that connected Cincinnati to Kentucky. We walked around the concourse to the Crosley Terrace, named after the Reds old ballpark, Crosley Field. We later stopped in the Reds Hall of Fame museum. Our Phillies hats were soaked from the rain, but I was just happy that they played the game. We took our group picture right behind home plate. The

Phillies won that game 4-2. I said to the guys, "We just completed the whole National League." As we were leaving the stadium, heading back to the hotel, Steve said to us, "29 frigging stadiums." I responded, "I can't believe we're one away, boys, next year we'll finish it out and we'll be in elite baseball company as fans."

The Phillies finished that season at 81-81, good for third place in the National League East. Our streak of five consecutive division titles and playoff appearances came to an end. The Phillies core players were getting older and worn down by injuries as the seasons progressed. It seemed like the reset button was inevitable on our 2008 World Champsionship squad.

Home of the Texas Rangers

Jay, Steve, Pat and Me at The Ballpark in Arlington, TX

Dealey Plaza in Dallas, TX

Texas School Book Depository

Cowboy Stadium in Arlington, TX

Pat's Wedding on June 16th, 2012

Great American Ballpark in Cincinnati, OH

Jay, Pat, Steve & Me at Great American Ballpark

Phillies vs Reds at Great American Ballpark

Fountain Square in Cincinnatti

The Final Out

On May 18th, 2013 we traveled to Minneapolis, Minnesota for our stadium finale trip. The month before, Pat and his wife had visited Busch Stadium in St. Louis. That was the one he was missing since 2008. Our flight landed in the area around 12 pm. We took a train from the airport over to the Mall of America. We were in awe of its size. I couldn't believe they had a full amusement park inside. Children were lining up outside each ride, begging their parents to stay 15 more minutes. Jay and Pat rode the humongous green roller coaster like young kids, without a care in world. It reminded me of summers in Wildwood, NJ. People screamed and hollered after every loop and turn on the coaster. The sounds of games and rides were loud in the background. I told the guys, "Let's grab something to eat in this huge food court, and then we can check into the hotel." We took the train to downtown Minneapolis.

Our hotel had a gym and a full basketball court inside, just like our hotel in Arizona had. The basketball created echoes throughout the gym every time it hit the hardwood floor. I had sweat pouring off my head, as I was gasping for air. I said, "I'm too old for this shit anymore." "Watch that damn knee," Steve said. I was set to have my second surgery in three years on my bad left knee. We continued to play basketball for another hour in the steaming-hot gym. We were soaked from top to bottom in sweat. Pat said, "Let's take showers and head over to Target Field. It's almost game time." After I caught my breath, I said, "Yeah that's a good idea; let's get ready to finish this out, boys."

It was 6pm and game time at Target Field. We realized that we had just accomplished something that most baseball fans only dream of. We had attended a game at every stadium in all of baseball. We walked around the concourse, and just laughed. "We had an amazing run here," the guys said. We took our traditional group photo down near the dugout. I remember patting the guys on the back, and saying, "We did it!" We shook hands, and said, "Job well done." We had never done that before throughout the entire journey. It just felt right. We honestly didn't care who won the game between the Twins and the Red Sox. We were there just to see Target Field, which opened three years earlier, in 2010. The outcome of the game was meaningless, because we felt like we had already won. I remember sitting in our seats, with a big smile on my face. I turned to the guys, and said, "What's next? They all just laughed. I said, "Let's do another sport?" Again, everyone just laughed. Ironically, three cast members from the movie "The Sandlot" were in attendance. That was one of our favorite baseball movies growing up. I said to the guys, "I feel like we just tackled the beast, after accomplishing all 30 stadiums."

Our goal was really to inspire other people to do this. I love when people tell me they're going to try to do it, because that's our favorite compliment. In the beginning it seemed impossible, and many times throughout I even doubted it. Anything is possible if you really want to do it. We always joke around, and say, "If anyone hits the lottery, we'll do it all over again." We hope that one day all of our kids get together and do the same thing. Baseball is a powerful sport, because for just a few hours, it clears your mind of what's going on in the world. Baseball brings the kid out of you, and brings people together.

The Phillies would finish the 2013 season at 73-89 good for 4th place in the National League East. They'd miss the playoffs for the second consecutive season, despite have one of the top payrolls in all of baseball. Manager Charile Manuel, who was the most successful coach in franchise history would be fired in August of that year. Ryan Sandberg would take over as interm coach for the reminder of the season.

On December 9th, 2013 Phillies ace Roy Halladay would retire and call it a career. Several nagging shoulder injuries caused him to lose control of his pitches and to no longer be an effective Major League pitcher. He had a brilliant career with both the Phillies and Blue Jays. He had won two Cy Young awards, and threw a perfect game and a no-hitter in the playoffs with the Phillies.

Target Field in Minneapolis, MN

Jay, Me, Pat & Steve at Target Field

Mall of America

The Mall of America Roller Coaster

Extra Innings We Go!

On May 10th, 2014 I finally married my longtime girlfriend Alana. Before the wedding, the guys wanted to take me out for a bachelor party. I told them I had something in mind. I wanted to return to Florida, to see the new Marlins Park. I said, "That stadium has been open since 2012, and it is time we saw it." We made arrangements in April to return to South Beach. "This is like a reunion!" I said. It was nice to have the crew back together again, almost a year after seeing our thirtieth stadium in Minnesota. Most of my groomsmen made the trip, which included my brother Mark, also my soon to be brother-in-law Eric, Steve's brother Bobby and of course Pat, Jay, and Steve. I was very excited for this final trip before tying the knot.

Our flight landed in sunny Miami, Florida on April 12th, 2014. South Beach was just as great as I remembered it to be. We stayed in the exact same condo from 2009. Ocean Drive was packed with people of all ages. Everyone was in their bathing suits just relaxing and soaking up the sun. People had their drinks in one hand, and a cigar or cigarette in the other. The guys said, "Let's hit the beach."

The sand was extra hot on that spring day in Florida. Back home in Philly it was in the 50's, and in Miami it was in the 80's. We approached the pretty blue water within seconds after we arrived on the beach. Besides the seaweed up front, it was picture-perfect. We all had cold drinks in our hands, without a care in the world. We put work in the back of our minds and fun in the front of them. I was extra stressed because of the wedding coming up, so I needed to relax that weekend. Later that night Pat found us a great steak house. We devoured our porterhouses, New York strips, and fillets. After dinner we went to Club Bed. It was a lounge at 8th and Ocean that you could just relax in, sitting on large beds and sofas. The music blasted and we partied until the early morning.

On April 14th, we prepared to see the new Marlins Park, which opened in 2012. The Marlins were hosting the Washington Nationals that Monday night. The stadium was enormous, and beautiful from the outside. They had a dome, due to their hot weather and their almost-daily rain showers. The palm trees swayed in the light Florida breeze. Ticket scalpers approached us as we walked up. I told the nice gentlemen that we had our tickets already, thank you. I could instantly feel the cold air conditioning on my hot red skin from the beach earlier that day. It reminded me of Tampa Bay, Houston and

Toronto, because of their domes. The stadium was huge. It was filled with brand new blue seats. The outfield walls were bright green. They had a large Marlins display in center field. It would go off every time a Marlins player homered. It reminded us of the Apple in Shea Stadium, or the train in Minute Maid Park, or the Liberty Bell in Citizens Bank Park. The smell of pizza, chicken, fries and steaks filled our noses, as we walked the large concourse. A bonus was that our tickets included "all you can eat", which was great. I swear I had five hot dogs and three sodas. Pat said, "You might die tonight." I laughed and said, "I don't even care because I've seen all 30 stadiums now." We found our seats behind home plate. There was a friendly usher, who gladly took our group picture. This was the best bachelor party I could ask for. I was spending it with my great friends at a baseball game in Miami. We enjoyed that trip, like we enjoyed every trip we did together. We laughed and reminisced about everything we had done throughout the years. We always joked, saying, "We felt like we were part of the teams." The Nationals beat the Marlins 9-2. I turned toward the guys, and said, "There's only one more place to visit, and that's the Hall of Fame."

The Phillies would finish the 2014 season in dead last at 73-89. The team clearly needed to rebuild and move on from the championship team roster. On July 31st, 2014 veteran southpaw pitcher Cliff Lee, the former Cy Young and fan favorite would make his final start in his amazing career. Lee had a number of elbow injuries that would keep him sidelined for the rest of 2014, and all of 2015. On December 14th, 2014 the Phillies traded long-time shortstop Jimmy Rollins to the Los Angeles Dodgers.

In 2015, the Phillies would part ways with the World Series MVP Cole Hamels. Hamels threw a no-hitter in his final start with the Phillies vs the Cubs at Wrigley Field. Just a few weeks later, The Phillies traded fan favorite, and possibly the greatest second basemen in team history, Chase Utley, to the Los Angeles Dodgers. Only Ryan Howard and Carlos Ruiz would remain as the only two players left from the 2008 World Series team. The Phillies would finish the 2015 season with a record of 63-99 as the worst team in baseball. We went from first to worst in just a few seasons. Manager Ryan Sandberg would resign as skipper, and Phillies GM Ruben Amaro, Jr would be fired.

On November 7th, 2015 Jay became the third member of our team to get married. We celebrated his special day together and partied all night long. We still joke to this day and say, "I can't believe we're married and we're 30 years old." I think I'm more shocked that we did 30 ballparks by the age of 30. Jay still has three more ballparks to do. We have every intention of helping him reach his goal too in the future.

Marlins Park in Miami, FL

Pat, Jay, Steve & Me at Marlins Park on my Bachelor Party

Marlins Park

My brother Mark, Jay, Me, Steve & Pat in Miami

My Wedding Day on 5/10/14

Jay's Wedding Day on 11/7/15

Call to the Hall

On March 12, 2016, almost three years after completing our 30th baseball trip, we finally decided to visit the Baseball Hall of Fame in Cooperstown, NY. We braced ourselves for a four-and-a-half hour road trip to upstate New York. We left South Philly and jumped on Interstate 76 around 11am that Saturday morning. Along the way we saw plenty of pretty scenery, going through Pennsylvania and New York State. During the ride we talked about previous trips, and discussed our plan for the upcoming weekend. We arrived in Cooperstown at approximately 4pm, then checked into our hotel. After dropping off our bags and quickly using the restroom, it was off to Main Street. Historic Main Street is only a few blocks long, and only consists of one traffic light. Just in sight was Doubleday Field, named after Abner Doubleday, who is credited with inventing the game of baseball. Doubleday was a United States Army officer and a Union General in the Civil War. Some people do doubt that Doubleday invented baseball. Doubleday Field hosted the Hall of Fame game from 1940-2008. We squeezed through the gate and onto the field. Pat said, "We should have brought our gloves and cleats." I took a picture, then proceeded down Main Street.

We immediately noticed how quiet and peaceful the area was. We assumed that was due to the fact that it was March, and baseball didn't start for another month. Jay said, "It's like a ghost town here." I replied, "You could hear a pin drop." We noticed many baseball-themed and vintage shops. Most of them sold new and old sports memorabilia, including stadium seats, cards, jerseys, and custom baseball bats. I walked into Cooperstown Bat Company, and saw many different types of lumber. I finally decided I wanted to get one engraved with all our names on it. I asked the guys what I should put on it. Pat responded, "30 Stadium Club." I liked that. Steve & Jay replied, "How about the years we traveled? 2006-2013?" which I also really liked. I spoke with the lady in the store, who said it would take around an hour to do, and that it would cost $75; I agreed. After I received the final product, I noticed Pat's name was spelled Leppo, not Lerro, on it. I kind of giggled when I saw it, but I was also a little pissed at the same time. I did just pay money for it. Steve saw it, and couldn't wait to show Jay, who immediately busted out laughing. We needed a nice laugh after the long ride up, plus we were starving. After 20 minutes further wait, she corrected the bat and we returned to Main Street.

Eventually, we had a nice dinner at Toscana Italian Grill & Bar. It had a cozy and small-town feel to it. The young busboy delivered us some warm bread, as the waiter took our orders. I had my usual chicken parmesan, and the guys had pasta dishes. Later on that night, we found a small pub just off Main Street to drink at. The bar had many locals in it, some shooting pool while others played darts. College basketball was playing on the television as March Madness approached. We sipped on our drinks and talked about visiting the museum the next day.

The next morning, we got up nice and early to have a filling breakfast at the Cooperstown Diner. It was located on Main Street, just a block away from the Hall of Fame. We could smell the fresh coffee and breakfast in the air, which just made us hungrier. It was a very small place, and only sported a handful of tables. It had an old-fashioned feel to it. We chose to sit at the counter, and ordered our food. I had a ham and cheese omelet, while the guys had pancakes with sausage, and some coffee. We talked about how the locals probably ate there on most mornings. We then began talking about what we were looking forward to in the museum. After we were done eating, we paid our check, then thanked and tipped the waitress. The next stop was the Baseball Hall of Fame.

The Hall of Fame was opened on June 12, 1939 by Stephen Carlton Clark. He was the owner of a small hotel in Cooperstown. Clark wanted to bring in tourists to help a city hurt and beaten as a result of The Great Depression and Prohibition.

As we approached the doors, I couldn't help but snap a few pictures. That was always one of my favorite things to do, and in a way was my job. As we walked in, I noticed the big glass doors. Once inside, I saw the big floor mats that said Hall of Fame. The guys said, "Watch him! He might take one for his basement." The middle-aged lady at the desk said, "The admission price is $23 dollars." We handed her the money and she gave us our ticket stubs and guides for the day. We were looking forward to seeing baseball immortality. The guys all joked with me, and said, "Keep the stub!" as they know I'm a huge collector of everything. The lady then told us to start on the second floor, which was the timeline of baseball. As we walked up the spiral staircase, I quickly noticed many artifacts from the 1800's and the beginning of baseball. I really enjoyed the Babe Ruth memorabilia, which included game balls, gloves, bats, and his actual Yankees uniform. Every kid wanted to grow up to be the "Great Bambino," and hit a home run like the great slugger from the Bronx did.

Next up was the stadium section, which made my eyes light up. There were actual stadium seats from Shibe Park, later named Connie Mack Stadium. I sat in them, and felt like I was watching a game on 21st & Lehigh, in North Philadelphia. I had Pat take some pictures of me in those and in seats from Veterans Stadium, the place that had introduced me to this great game in South Philadelphia. Finally, we walked through the halls with all of the players' plaques from over the years. Many I had never heard of before, but many I recognized quickly. As we exited, I tried to take time to really take it all in, to enjoy what we just experienced. Shortly after leaving the museum, we hopped back in the car and got ready to head back to Philadelphia. On the ride home we reminisced about all of the stadium trips, and all of the crazy adventures we'd been through, including ones yet to come. We plan on visiting every new ballpark as it opens. We already plan to attend a game at Sun Trust Stadium in Atlanta in 2017.

The Baseball Hall of Fame

Doubleday Field in Cooperstown, NY

Shibe Park seats in the Hall of Fame

Veterans Stadium seats in the Hall of Fame

Inside the Hall of Fame

The Cooperstown Diner on Main Street

The Last Pitch

S ince the first time I stepped inside Veterans Stadium back in 1994 as I kid, I knew I loved this game. There's something about the sound a bat makes when it hits the ball, or the way the crowd roars after a big home run. There's something special about the way a catcher's glove pops after a pitcher throws a fastball 100 mph, or the excitement in a umpires voice when he rings a player up for strike three. The special smell of roasted peanuts and Cracker Jack. There's no clock in baseball, unlike other sports. It's over when it's over, similar to life. Baseball lets you escape reality for just a few hours. It's something the whole family can enjoy, at all ages. It's a special game from first pitch until the final out each night.

Major League Baseball is heading in the right direction as we speak. Attendance numbers are through the roof, as are television deals in the billions. Many bright stars fill the junior and senior circuits, such as young all-stars Mike Trout, Bryce Harper, and Kris Bryant. The steroid era in baseball is well in the rear-view mirror and pitching is more dominated than ever. Many of the players I grew up watching in the 90's are now in the Hall of Fame. It was a great era of baseball for me to grow up in and learn the game.

The Philadelphia Phillies are now in complete rebuild mode. We're hoping that they are competitive again by 2018. We'll never forget the success we had through the glory years from 2007-2011, when we had won five straight division titles, two National League Pennants, and one World Series title.

Curtain Call

I want to thank everyone who supported us throughout this adventure. I especially want to thank my travel mates and close friends Steven Grosso, Pat Lerro, and Jason Pinto for letting me experience baseball like this. I want to thank my wife Alana, and Pat's wife Jackie for putting up with us while we slept away from home for so many weekends of the year.

I want to thank all of the pilots, cab drivers, and train conductors in every city or state who helped us safely reach our destination every time. I want to thank all of the hotels, restaurants, and stadiums that we visited for their kindness, friendliness, and hospitality.

I want to thank my editor Chadd Paul Davidson for his work on this book. I also want to thank you, the reader, for purchasing or downloading this book. I hope you enjoyed the ride as we did. This was our story, now go make yours!

Our Top 5 Favorite Stadiums

Stephen
AT&T Park

PNC Park

Oriole Park

Fenway Park

Petco Park

Jay
PNC Park

Petco Park

AT&T Park

Minute Maid Park

Marlins Park

Pat
PNC Park

Petco Park

Citizens Bank Park

AT&T Park

Fenway Park

Steve
Fenway Park

Wrigley Field

Petco Park

Citizens Bank Park

Dodger Stadium

The Road Trip Scouting Report

We decided to space out 30 stadiums over the course of 7 baseball seasons, to really get to experience each city. Still, for the sake of saving time and money, we decided to do some of the stadium city trips together, like San Diego and Los Angeles, and Chicago and Milwaukee. You too could do the same to make your 30 MLB stadium trips memorable, here's how:

1. **Start local!** If you've already been to Citizens Bank Park for the Phillies, you're already plus one out of the possible 30. You could begin by going to all the drivable MLB stadiums in the area: Washington Dc, Baltimore, New York Yankees, Mets, Pittsburgh and Boston.

2. **Fly away!** Start wherever you, like but plan in advance and use apps that track airfare prices for you, like "Hopper" on iOS, then book when you see prices at their lowest.

3. **Pair stadiums up!** Washington and Baltimore home the same weekend? Stay in either city and hit up a game each day. You could also do both New York and Chicago teams, based on their schedule. Also worth the train ride along the Pacific coast is heading to San Diego's stadium and then taking the train up to Anaheim, home of the Los Angeles Angels.

4. **Enjoy it!** Whether with family or friends, each city is a unique experience. If you're only there in a city for say 48 hours, plan in advance and see what the city has to offer that interests you, and put it on your itinerary for the trip. **By Pat Lerro.**

Stephen Pagano

Philadelphia Row Home Magazine

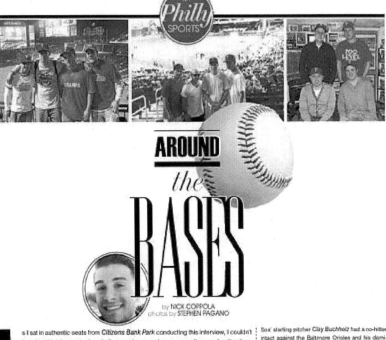

AROUND *the* BASES

by NICK COPPOLA
photos by STEPHEN PAGANO

s I sat in authentic seats from *Citizens Bank Park* conducting this interview, I couldn't help but think I was at a baseball game. I scanned my surroundings and noticed authentic stadium seats from other baseball stadiums. Sports memorabilia hung on the walls or was propped neatly in a corner of the room. Finally, my eyes came across a row of pictures bordering the entire top half of the back basement wall.

I asked my friend Stephen Pagano why he had basically the same picture of the same four guys displayed along the wall.

"My friends Pat, Joe, Steve and I visited all 30 MLB stadiums and those are pictures of us at all of them," he answered.

This is the story of *Stephen Pagano, Pat Lerro, Steven Grosso and Jason Pinto* and their adventures traveling the country to visit every MLB stadium. Four childhood friends from South Philadelphia who share a passionate love for the game of baseball and all it has to offer in a lifetime.

The long journey started with a night trip to the old Yankee Stadium in 2006. The Yankees were playing the Red Sox that day in a classic AL East rivalry game. At this point in time, the guys did not have their goal in mind yet.

"The environment in New York was intense and exciting," Grosso says. "Seeing a rivalry like that was a lot of fun to experience."

Little did the four know, that one day in New York would have a huge impact on their lives for years to follow. After arriving home from *Yankee Stadium*, the guys decided to plan road trips to closer stadiums on the East coast starting the following season. Their original plans were to hit the most historic baseball

stadiums first. Trips to Camden Yards in Baltimore, Yankee Stadium, Shea Stadium in New York, Fenway Park in Boston and Wrigley Field in Chicago closed out the 2007 baseball season for the quartet. Still, the group didn't have their ultimate goal set in stone while touring those five stadiums.

However, that one September night in Boston would change the mindset of the group going forward. It was the sixth inning and Jason Pinto's eyes lit up as he glanced at the old-school style scoreboard displayed along the "green monster" in left field. Without actually saying any words, he directed his friends' attention to the scoreboard so they would also realize what was taking place. The Red

Sox' starting pitcher *Clay Buchholz* had a no-hitter intact against the Baltimore Orioles and his dominance continued as it got later in the game.

"I didn't want to jinx the no-hitter but I wanted the guys to know what was going on without saying the words," Pinto explains.

Finally, the last out of the game was recorded and the crowd erupted with claps and cheers for their hometown pitcher. Buchholz finished the game with a no-hitter!

"The no-hitter at Fenway really compelled us to start planning more trips," Grosso says. "Experiencing something that unique was a sign that we need to continue traveling to other baseball stadiums."

"It was the first time I heard a stadium that loud in my life," Pagano says. "We were jumping up and down like our team won the World Series. Little did we know the Phillies would go on to win it all just a year later."

With the conclusion of the 2007 season, the group decided they were going to tour the country and visit every MLB stadium the league had to offer. It was final, the goal was set and 24 stadiums remained as the 2008 season rolled around.

Like many kids growing up in the city, the four friends acquired their love for the game of baseball at a young age. They played little league baseball, watched baseball movies like *Rookie of the Year* and *The Sandlot* and mimicked their favorite players' batting stances while playing up the street.

Volume 31 Issue 41

"We were so close to the stadium that we were able to join in on the experience even though we weren't actually at the game"

All four guys recall watching the Phillies play the Toronto Blue Jays in the 1993 World Series. Even though they were young at the time, they still understood the magnitude of the game and were glued to the TV during these games.

"When Joe Carter hit the homerun for us to lose the series, that's when it all started for me. It got me interested," Pagano says.

Veterans Stadium was perhaps most instrumental in bringing baseball to the forefront of their interests during their childhood. The crew spent most of their summer days at the complex getting autographs in the afternoon from the players as they pulled their cars into the stadium parking lot and then going to the game at night.

"I grew up at the Vet in the 700 level. It was all I knew," Pagano says. "Some kids went down the shore, some kids went to summer camp. What I did was go to the Vet all summer to watch Lenny Dykstra, Darren Daulton and Mickey Morandini play baseball."

Steven Grosso remembers watching the fireworks and being able to hear the cheers from the Vet while standing on his doorstep.

"We were so close to the stadium that we were able to join in on the experience even though we weren't actually at the game," Grosso says. "Picture watching the game on TV and seeing someone hit a homerun. Then you open your front door and hear the roar of the crowd like you're actually at the stadium watching the game live."

The quartet agrees that without those experiences at the Vet growing up, they probably wouldn't have had the drive to complete the goal of traveling to all 30 stadiums. It paved the way for all of them.

Each member of the group played an important role in traveling all over the country. Steve Pagano booked most of the trips, looking for good prices on airfare and hotels. Pat Lerro was the itinerary guy. He made sure local restaurants, bars and sightseeing attractions were lined up once the crew arrived in a new city.

"Since we were only going to be there for a short period of time, I wanted to get the best experience in each city," Lerro says.

Steve Grosso was the blueprint man devising strategies to get the most out of the city before or after the game. Lastly, Jason Pinto added the positive energy to help mesh the guys into a perfect group.

"We treated it like we were a general manager of a baseball team in the sense that we had to manage our money and look for the best deals available," Pagano says.

It was definitely a group effort. Their desire to keep pushing toward their goal made booking these trips a little easier. Everyone was on board no matter what time of the year it was. Steve Pagano jokes about being in Toronto on July 4th during our own country's Independence Day to see the Phillies play the Blue Jays in the Rogers Centre.

When the journey began, the guys visited the stadiums regardless of who the home team was playing that day. But with the Phillies taking the league by storm in 2008, they decided it was time to try and visit those stadiums while the Phillies were in town.

The adventure became troublesome once the guys completed all the stadiums that were within driv-

ing distance. The crew then had to book flights to the Midwest and West Coast stadiums, which became a little pricey. But that wasn't discouraging them from accomplishing their ultimate goal.

Steve Pagano admits that he didn't think it was possible to make it to all 30 stadiums until he had a conversation with a man sitting next to him on a flight to San Diego. The man had been to 20 stadiums himself and was interested in hearing Steve's travel experiences.

"I told him that we had visited 12 stadiums so far and were on our way to Petco Park in San Diego to complete another one," Pagano says. "He then gave us the idea to go to Angels Stadium in Los Angeles the same weekend we were in San Diego. Right there, I knew it was destiny. Doing two stadiums on one trip changed everything and we ended up doing that multiple times."

Traveling experiences were not always smooth sailing. The guys agree that their trip to Progressive Field in Cleveland and Comerica Park in Detroit was the craziest weekend trip they ever experienced. First they had to drive from Philadelphia to Baltimore. Then they had to take a flight out of Baltimore to Cleveland to watch the game.

The following morning, they rushed to the bus station to take a Greyhound bus from Cleveland to Detroit. After watching the game in Detroit, they had to fly back to Baltimore to eventually drive back home to Philadelphia. Whew!

"Cleveland and Detroit were most definitely the most grueling travel experiences of the whole trip," Lerro says.

The guys had to pack lightly using just a backpack so they could get into the stadiums without any trouble. Sometimes, they only got a couple hours of sleep. The Cleveland/Detroit weekend marked their 20th stadium with only 10 more to go.

Each has a different favorite stadium for a number of different reasons. Pat and Jason liked PNC Park in Pittsburgh because of the skyline hovering behind the centerfield fence. Steve Pagano's favorite was Camden Yards in Baltimore because of the shape and dimensions of the stadium and its impact on ballparks of the future. Steve Grosso enjoyed Fenway Park in Boston because of its history and the feel of it during a game.

"When you're there, it's just a great experience," Grosso says. "If you're a baseball fan, I think you should experience Fenway Park. You really can't explain it until you see for yourself."

All four guys decided that St. Louis had the best fans – hands down. The crew said only good things about the Cardinal fans calling them the most respectful and knowledgeable fans of the game of baseball. They actually thanked us for coming to the stadium to visit."

However, the crew stressed that our own Philadelphia fans are the most passionate.

Even though the ultimate goal was to make it to all 30 MLB stadiums, that didn't stop the guys from enjoying what each city had to offer.

"We tried to see or do at least one main thing that was relevant to the city we were visiting," Pinto says.

Pat made sure there was at least one attraction in each city for the group to check out. Some of their favorites were Dealey Plaza in Dallas, the Golden

Gate Bridge and Alcatraz in San Francisco and the Hollywood sign. Many memories were made during their journey. Simple things like sipping an ice cold Coors Light at Coors Field or a Miller Lite at Miller Park. And driving around California in a gold convertible. The guys took in everything and enjoyed the whole adventure.

To top it all off, they experienced this quest during perhaps the best stretch of success in Phillies baseball history.

"The Phillies were so good at the time, it pumped our egos up a little more when opposing fans would heckle us for wearing our Phillies attire," Pinto says.

At the beginning of the 2013 season, only one stadium remained. On May 18, 2013, the guys set out for Target Field in Minnesota. The last destination of their journey. As the final out was recorded, it marked the end of a seven-year escapade among four friends from South Philadelphia.

"When the game was over, it was a bittersweet feeling," Grosso says. "To everybody else in attendance, it was a routine baseball game. But for us, it was unique. It was the end of our journey."

"We actually shook hands outside of the stadium when it was over, something we've never done before during the whole thing," Lerro says. "It was a symbolization of a job well-done for all of us."

The group started this trek in their early 20s and it helped them grow as individuals without them even realizing it. Through all the memories and experiences, they learned important life lessons. Like getting out of your comfort zone. And if you believe in something and put your mind to it, anything is possible. They even got to experience how other people live outside of Philadelphia.

"We were opened up to the rest of America," Lerro says.

"It was an educating experience," Grosso agrees. "It's nice to have a journey we can call our own."

"We got to see things most people dream about," Pagano says.

Some of the stadiums they visited differ quite a bit from Citizens Bank Park, they say. There are a lot of features inside Citizens Bank Park that are unique to Philadelphia. Grosso says, "Things like the Liberty Bell and cheesesteaks."

"Citizens Bank Park is home. It just feels right. This is where we're supposed to be," Pinto says.

With the Phillies franchise going through a rebuilding stage for the next few seasons, the guys just want to see some progression from our younger players and be able to watch some good baseball games.

As far as future travel plans, the friends are planning more trips like the one they took to the Baseball Hall of Fame in Cooperstown, New York. They look forward to seeing the new Sun Trust Stadium when it opens in Atlanta.

"Our goal now is to visit every new MLB stadium that opens up," Pagano says.

As they reminisce about their past adventure, they say it's hard to believe that they accomplished their goal and visited all 30 stadiums, an experience that no one can take from them. Regrets? Not one. In fact, they say they'd do it all over again if they got the chance. ▦

We were featured in the April 2016 edition.

Stephen Pagano

<u>United We Stand</u>

The Statue of Liberty

2008 World Series Champions

2009 National League Champions

Stephen Pagano

<u>RIP- Harry Kalas</u>

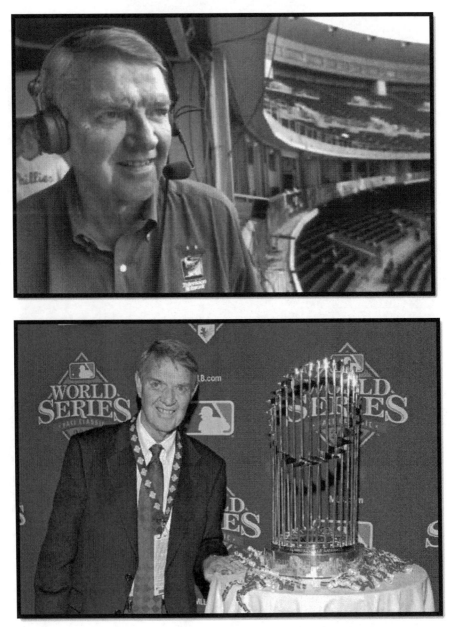

1936-2009

Around the Bases

Also check out Around the Bases written by Steven Grosso.

About the Author

Stephen Pagano is married and lives in South Philadelphia. He's been a baseball fan his whole life and has seen a game at 34 different baseball stadiums. Any questions, comments, or concerns about this book can be directed to stephenpagano30by30@yahoo.com.

32781673R00123

Made in the USA
Middletown, DE
17 June 2016